THE 365 FUNNIEST

Golf Jokes

THE 365 FUNNIEST

Golf Jokes

Compiled by Fred Gefen

A Citadel Press Book
Published by Carol Publishing Group

Carol Publishing Group Edition, 1999

A Citadel Press Book
Published by Carol Publishing Group
Citadel Press is a registered trademark of Carol Communications, Inc.

Editorial, sales and distribution, rights and permissions inquiries
should be addressed to Carol Publishing Group, 120 Enterprise Avenue,
Secaucus, N.J. 07094

In Canada: Canadian Manda Group, One Atlantic Avenue, Suite 105,
Toronto, Ontario M6K 3E7

Carol Publishing Group books may be purchased in bulk at special
discounts for sales promotions, fund-raising, or educational purposes.
Special editions can be created to specifications. For details, contact
Special Sales Department, Carol Publishing Group, 120 Enterprise Avenue,
Secaucus, N.J. 07094

Manufactured in the United States of America
15 14 13 12 11 10 9 8 7 6 5

Library of Congress Cataloging-in-Publication Data

Gefen, Fred
    365 funniest golf jokes / compiled by Fred Gefen.
        p. cm.
    "A Citadel Press book."
    ISBN 0-8065-1688-7
    1. Golf—Humor. I. Title.
PN6231.G48G44 1995
818'.5402—dc20   95-9370
                                                    CIP

For Randi and Taylor Michelle.
My loves, my life.

Golf Jokes

*The worst day of golf is infinitely better
than the best day of work.*

Tee Off

● ● ●

It all started innocently enough. I was out one day, hacking up yet another poor defenseless golf course when suddenly the thought came to me. "What a joke!" I said to myself. Although at the time I was commenting on the typically stellar quality of my golf game, for some strange reason, it also came to me at that moment, Lord only knows why, that what the world needed was a book of golf jokes and that I was going to be the one to write it. Right then and there, whenever then and wherever there was, my life had new meaning. I was on a mission. My mission was to put together the *definitive* collection of golf humor. It quickly became my own private little *Field of Divots*. You know, kind of like "Write It And They Will Come." Anyway, little at that time did I fully grasp the size of the task I had put before myself. It seemed unending. So many jokes, so little time. I became obsessive in my quest. Just ask any of my friends. The one plus, of course, was that I didn't have to give up any time on the golf course. It was a *huge* plus, actually. (Hey, I was obsessed. I wasn't stupid.)

All over the world came the rallying cry, "Heard any good golf jokes lately?" Luckily for me, a lot of people had, and were kind enough to take the time to share. This book is dedicated to all those nice folks who had the patience and good will to stop whatever they were doing at the time (usually attempting to hit a golf ball) and aid me in my quest.

Also, a special thanks to my buddy, Palmer (no, not Arnold), last year's leading money winner on the Peanut Butter Tour, and one of the original "Iron Man" golfers, without whose technical input and assistance, this book would have been a lot more difficult to complete.

So here they are. Some are old, some are new, some are borrowed, none are *too* blue. I sincerely hope they make you smile. Please feel free to pass them on. Who knows, maybe you'll set someone laughing so hard, they'll miss a short putt and you'll make some money. But more important, here's hoping all your drives find the fairway and all your putts find the cup. Have fun!

1

A fellow was out on a golf course that bordered a farm playing a round of golf with his wife when they came to the seventh hole. Now, the seventh hole at this particular course was a long par four with a dogleg to the right that happened to go around a barn. The man took his driver out of his bag, set up over the ball, and proceeded to dub his tee shot, knocking it almost straight up into the air. It landed about 100 yards down the fairway. Needing about 200 yards just to carry the dogleg, he was, needless to say, not in particularly good shape. However, upon reaching the ball, he noticed the barn to his right and had a brainstorm. Why couldn't he guide his second shot *through* the barn to get to the green?

Armed with this little bit of inspiration, he sent his wife over to the barn with the instructions to open the front and rear doors, thus giving him a clear shot at the green. His wife did as he requested, opening both doors and standing off to the side in the barn as her husband pulled out his trusty, old three wood and took aim. He took the club back and blasted a low liner that miraculously headed straight through the front door of the barn.

Unfortunately, through the front door was about as far as it got. The ball never made it out the back. Instead, it ricocheted off one of the posts in the barn, crashing into the side of his wife's head, killing her instantly.

Fade to one year later. The fellow is out on the same course for the first time since the horrible accident, this time with one of the caddies from the club. They arrive at the seventh hole and once again he flubs his tee shot, and it doesn't make the dogleg. He just sighs.

"Don't be too concerned, sir. I have an idea," says the caddie. "Why don't I go over to that barn over there and open the doors so you can shoot through it to get to the green?"

"No, no," says the man, "I can't do that"

"Why not?" asked the caddie.

"I tried that a year ago," he said, "...and it cost me three strokes!"

2

Abe had been married to the same woman for over forty years, and in all that time he had never lied to her about anything. She wasn't crazy about his playing golf, but she tolerated it as long as he made the time to take her to do the things she needed to do. Well, one day he finished playing his usual eighteen holes of golf and was heading home to pick up his wife to take her to an appointment. As he drove through the club parking lot, he noticed a beautiful young woman standing alone with a very distressed look on her face. Being a gentleman, Abe pulled over to where the woman was standing, rolled down his window and asked if there was anything he could do to help.

"My friend was supposed to pick me up here, and I've been waiting for more than forty-five minutes," she said. "It doesn't look like she's going to show. I don't know how I'm going to get home."

"Perhaps I can offer you a ride?" suggested Abe. "I'd be more than happy to drop you off."

"That would be very sweet of you. I'd appreciate it," she said and hopped into the car and off they went.

They arrived at her house, and Abe pulled the car into the driveway.

"I can't begin to thank you enough for bringing me home," she said, "but as long as you're already here, why don't you come in for a few minutes and let me fix you a drink?"

Abe thought about it (maybe for half a second) and figured what would be the harm in having a quick drink? So he turned off the car, and they went inside.

Well, wouldn't you know that one thing led to another, and four hours later Abe comes walking out of this woman's house with the world's biggest case of the guilties. He had done a *bad* thing, and now he had to face the music. To say he was beside himself was the understatement of the year. What in the world was he going to tell his wife? The whole way home he was busy concocting in his mind all kinds of different stories he could tell her, until he realized he'd never be able to pull it off. He decided the only thing he could do was to tell her the truth. He owed her that much. Besides, he figured, after all these years of marriage, he was sure she'd understand and find it in her heart to forgive him. He hoped.

He arrived home, pulled the car into the garage, unloaded his clubs, and went into the house to find his wife waiting for him in the kitchen. She stared blankly at him as he hung his head and related the story of the girl in the parking lot, the ride home, and the innocent invitation that turned into something much more. When he finished his story, he raised his head to see her looking at him with a rage in her eyes he had never seen before. He was a dead man.

"How *dare* you lie to me?!" she shouted. *"You played thirty-six holes!!!"*

3

Two well-heeled women were about to tee off at their country club one morning, when one turned to the other.

"Tell me, darling," she said, "before we head off, shall we play men's rules... or does every shot count?"

4

Once upon a time, there was a man who loved to play golf. He had, however, one small problem. Every time he'd stand over a short putt he'd become flatulent, and the really strange thing about this was that whenever he became flatulent, it would sound exactly like the word "Honda." While he obviously found this to be most disconcerting, he so loved the game that he just tried his best to ignore the problem. As you can probably imagine, this was no small task.

Anyway, one day he took a business trip to Japan. After wrapping up his business, he accepted an offer from his Japanese associates to join them for a round of golf before heading home. He was, of course, mindful of his little problem, but golf being what it is in Japan, he didn't want to insult his associates by refusing their offer.

Sure enough, on the very first green, his problem reared its ugly head. He became flatulent and it sounded just like "Honda." He became quite embarrassed, and as he attempted to apologize to his partners, one of them said, "No need to worry. We know of most honorable doctor who can solve your problem. When we finish game, we will give you his number in Tokyo, and you will go see him. He will take care of you."

Willing to try anything at this point, our man agreed. When they finished, he took the doctor's number, called, and made an appointment for the next day.

Arriving at the doctor's office the next day at the appointed hour, he was led into an examining room. A few minutes later, the doctor came into the room, introduced himself, and asked what the problem was. After explaining his situation, the doctor said, "No problem, we fix you right up. Hop up here on table."

Up on the table he hopped, and after a rather detailed examination, the doctor proudly proclaimed, "I know what your problem is."

"You do?" said our guy. "What is it?"

"You have abscess," said the doctor.

"I have an abscess?" he said.

"Correct," said the doctor. "You have abscess."

"What in the world does an abscess have to do with my condition?"

"Don't you know?" said the doctor. "*Abscess Makes the Fart Go Honda!*"

5

Jim was having a horrid day out on the links. No matter what he did, he just couldn't make a shot. He finally got to the point where he couldn't take it anymore, and he started tossing his clubs. And we're not talking tossing them down the fairway. Every time he missed shot, he'd take the offending golf club and either fling it into the nearest water hazard, or else he'd break it over his leg. He finally got to the point where he'd thrown away his last club and finding himself in a rather awkward situation, he turned to his caddie and asked, "What do I do now?"

His caddie, who to this point had watched silently as this little spectacle unfolded, thought a moment, kind of shrugged his shoulders, and said, "I really don't know, sir, but might I inquire if you'll be needing that sweater?"

6

Dave's boss was becoming more and more annoyed as Dave continued to take days off from work for one death in the family after the next. You'd think this guy had the world's biggest and sickest family. Knowing what the real deal was, the boss had enough one day, and he called Dave into his office.

"You know Dave," he began, "I wish we could somehow get you to care about your work here as much as you obviously care about golf."

"I don't know, sir," replied Dave, "I could *never* take work that seriously."

7

There's a rumor that Marilyn Monroe once yelled "Fore" on a golf course...and *thirty* came running!

8

One woman was commenting to her friend, "I haven't seen my husband in over eleven years."

"Lucky you," said her friend." "He must have taken up golf."

9

"So how did it go at the golf course today?" the fellow asked his six-months-pregnant wife as she came in the door.

"How did it go?" she asked. "It went great. I played so well that when I walked off the eighteenth green, I actually felt the baby applaud!"

10

"You know, I always wondered," a fellow asked his golfing partners one day, "where do you suppose is the safest place to be when you call up the foursome behind you on a par three?"

"That's an easy one," responded one of his pals. "Right next to the hole, of course."

11

Once upon a time, a real hacker challenged his country club's golf pro to a round of golf for a sizable amount of money.

The match was to be stroke play, even up, with no handicap for the hacker. The hacker, however, did manage to have included a stipulation that during the course of the round he was to receive two "Gotcha's."

To just about everyone at the club, this seemed like a wonderful chance to make some easy money, and needless to say, the side betting leaned almost exclusively toward the pro.

The day of the big match came, and back in the clubhouse it was reported that the hacker had finished the round with a 106. This caused a lot of people to start counting their money until the news came in that, almost unbelievably, the pro had shot a 107. A stunned silence came over the room that probably would have continued indefinitely had not the pro entered the clubhouse looking pretty much like it was the end of the world.

"What in the world happened out there?" asked one of the shocked members (obviously, one who had bet on the pro). "How could you have possibly let him beat you?"

The pro paused a moment, let out a small sigh, and began his tale.

"We walked up to the first tee and he hit first. He sliced his tee shot, and I remember thinking to myself that this was going to be like taking candy from a baby. I teed up my ball, and just as I was about to hit, he sneaks up behind me, slams his driver up between my legs and yells 'Gotcha!' It was all over from there. I couldn't play golf. I spent the entire round waiting for the second 'Gotcha'."

12

A couple from up North recently moved to the Dallas, Texas, area. The first thing they did when they arrived was to apply for membership at the ritziest, most expensive private golf club in the area that, as it happened, had just hosted a P.G.A. event. They took a tour of the facilities, filled out and turned in their application, and were given an appointment to meet with the membership committee. The day of the meeting came, and the couple was understandably quite nervous. It was very important that they give a good impression to the committee if they were to be asked to join. They arrived at the club at the appointed hour and were led into an opulent conference room where the membership committee was already assembled and waiting for them. Things were going along quite well until one of the committee members posed a question to the wife.

"I'm sure everyone on this committee would like to know what you think of the great Sam Houston?" the committee member asked.

"I think he's great," the wife fudged, having absolutely no clue as to who Sam Houston was. "I was especially impressed by the way he got out of that bunker on the tenth hole at the tournament the other week."

As she said this, she glanced over to see her husband cringe and slump in his chair, and she realized that she must have committed a major faux pas.

As they left the club in their car, the wife finally said to her husband, "I'm so sorry, dear. I didn't mean to screw things up."

"I can't believe you did that," he snapped at her. "Don't you know anything? There *is no bunker* on the tenth hole!"

13

The manager of the pro shop was minding the store one quiet afternoon when, all of a sudden, one of the members came storming in the front door carrying the new set of clubs he had purchased the week before.

"Sam," says Ed, "we gotta talk."

"What do we gotta talk about, Ed?"

"We gotta talk about these clubs you sold me last week. They're defective."

"What do you mean they're defective?" asked Sam.

"What do you mean, 'What do I mean?' . . . I mean just what I said," said Ed. "The clubs are defective; they just don't work."

"Now, Ed, what makes you say that?" inquired Sam.

"It was obvious from the day that I got them that they were no good. The woods slice everything, the long irons only know how to hook, the short irons are totally incapable of hitting anything other than fat shots, and that putter—that putter couldn't make a putt if you dug a channel directly into the cup!"

14

After dessert, the women stayed around the kitchen table to chat, while the men went into the living room to talk. Soon, the conversation in the living room turned to the subject of golf.

"What was your best score?" one of the men asked another.

"Let me find out," he said, as he got up and started to head to the dining room.

"Where are you going?" they asked him.

"To find my wife," he said. "She's the only one who remembers what I've been telling people."

15

The golfer and his caddie had been out on the course for what seemed like forever. After more than several hours had gone by, the caddie began spending what, to the golfer, seemed to be an inordinate amount of time looking at his watch. The man was becoming annoyed at his caddie's actions and finally spoke up.

"I just want you to know," said the man, "that I'm aware that I'm not the world's greatest golfer. But even so, I've taken the day off and have no place to be, so I'm just going to relax and enjoy myself no matter how long it takes to finish. So you can stop constantly looking at your watch."

"I fully appreciate that fact, sir," said the caddie, "but this is not my watch, it's a compass."

16

A wife was complaining to her husband that he had been playing too much golf.

"I must tell you," she said to him, "if you ever were to stay at home on Sunday, I'd have a stroke and drop dead."

"What's that supposed to be," he asked, "a bribe?"

17

Two friends were sitting at the bar one evening talking about the sports they liked to participate in.

"I love to play golf," the first guy said. "I think it's the best sport to play."

"No way," said his friend. "I have a big problem with golf. There's something about it that's just not natural."

"Not natural?" the first guy said. "Golf not natural? How in the world could you possibly say something like that?"

"The way I see it," said his friend, "is that there's something just not right about a game where the person who gets the most hits, loses!"

18

The elderly golfer was complaining to one of his younger partners in the clubhouse one afternoon.

"I'm having all kinds of trouble getting out of those damn bunkers," he said.

"That's easy to correct," said his buddy, who proceeded to go into a long, drawn-out explanation of the finer points of bunker play. Open the stance, dig in with your feet, play the ball up in your stance, open the club face, hit behind the ball, you know, the works. This guy finally finishes the lesson, and he says to his friend,

"So does that cover it for you?"

"Yes, thank you, it would have if I had been talking about the ball. I was, however, talking about me!"

19

Satan called a staff meeting of all his demons and trolls.

"Things have gotten much too easy around here," he complained to the assembled crowd. "It's time we toughened things up, but we must be sneaky about it. I want there to be misery, but not just plain misery. I want the worst kind of misery. The kind of misery that offers with it a supreme false sense of hope that things may actually get better. Any suggestions?"

There was a long moment of silence until, all the way in the back of the cave, a little claw was raised above the crowd.

An ugly, gnarly little gnome stood up and said to Satan, "Your Great Vileness, why not make them play golf?"

20

Definition of polo: Golf with automatic fertilization.

21

A young man was brought to testify before the judge. The judge looked down over the bench at the fellow and said to him,
"Have you ever taken the oath before?"

The man just stood there with a blank expression on his face, so the judge repeated the question, which elicited the same response.

"Perhaps you didn't understand me," said the judge. "Do you know how to swear?"

With that, the young man's eyes widened and a smile came across his face. "Of course I know how to swear, Your Honor," he said. "You're the one who taught me how. Don't you recognize me? I'm your caddie."

22

Then there was the story about the woman golfer whose fairway shot struck a tree and bounced back at her, landing in her bra. Seems she took the penalty but was last heard absolutely refusing to play the ball from where it lay.

23

Two friends were out on the course one day. One of them was not having a good go of it and by the twelfth hole had lost all the golf balls he had in his bag. Undeterred, he simply began using his friend's balls and continued having no success. As he went into his friend's bag for about the fourth time, his friend had had quite enough.

"If you don't mind," he friend said, "how about being a little more careful with your shots? Those balls cost me over three dollars apiece."

"Listen," he snapped, "don't complain to me. If you can't afford to play this game, then you have no business being out here."

24

After church one Sunday, one of the congregants went up to the priest and said, "Father, is it a sin to play golf on Sunday?"

"My son," said the priest, putting his hand on the man's shoulder, "I've seen you play golf. It's a sin *any* day."

25

It was the first golfing day of the new season, and Rich couldn't wait to get out on the course. He'd spent the entire winter practicing indoors, working on his swing and his putting. He had even invested a small fortune to go to one of those Southern golf schools for an intensive two weeks of one-on-one instruction, and he was ready. He headed out with his caddie and around about the sixth hole he turned to the caddie who up until then hadn't had much to say, and, while puffing his chest out with pride, said to him, "So tell me, have you noticed anything different since last year?"

"Yes, sir," said the caddie, "I certainly have."

"And what's that," said the man, grinning.

"You've had your clubs regripped."

26

A man came before the judge for committing a minor traffic infraction. As he stood before the bench, he noticed the judge taking a long, hard look at him as if her were trying to recognize him.

"Don't I know you from somewhere?" asked the judge.

"Why yes, Your Honor, as it happens, you do," said the man with a smile on his face, certain that he was going to be let off the hook. "I'm the fellow that gave your wife golf lessons. Now do you remember me?"

"I most certainly do," said the judge. "I hereby sentence you to *thirty years!*"

27

Mark was heading out the door one morning on his way to the course, when his wife saw him passing through the kitchen.

"Gee, honey," she said, "you really look great. You've got the expensive sweater, stylish hat, nice crisp slacks and shirt, and smart-looking shoes. Your bag is lovely, the woods are gleaming, and the irons are shining. Yes sirree, you are really something to behold!"

"Why, thank you, sweetheart," he said, as he walked out the door.

"Oh, and by the way, honey," she said.

"What, dear?" he said, stopping in the doorway.

"It's too bad you're going to have to go and spoil it all by playing."

28

The hacker took his usual lousy tee shot, leaving himself a shot of about 275 yards just to get to the green. He arrived at the ball, took a brief glance down the fairway, walked over to his bag and pulled out his pitching wedge.

"Sir," exclaimed his caddie, looking in his yardage book,

"you're going to use *that* club for this shot. It's exactly 278 yards from here just to reach the front edge of the green."

"Listen," snapped the hacker, "if I had wanted a surveyor to come along with me today, I would have hired one!"

29

A group of archaeologists were out in the middle of the Sahara desert working on a site where a few ancient artifacts had been discovered. As they dug out the site, they came across an amazing discovery. They came upon what seemed to be the remains of a golf course, buried deep under the sand. The leaders of the expedition couldn't believe their luck, but as they continued to clear the site, it turned out to indeed be the remains of an ancient golf course. And if that weren't enough, near what they believed to be the first tee, they found a clay tablet with a very strange form of writing on it.

"Can you read it?" the chief of the expedition asked his local foreman. "I *must* know what it says."

"Yes, Sahib, I think I can," said the foreman.

"Well, quickly, man, get to it," said the chief.

The foreman took the tablets into his tent and was neither seen nor heard from for three days and three nights. Finally on the fourth morning, he emerged from his tent looking tired and worn, but he had cracked the language of the tablet.

"Tell me," said the chief, "what happened to these people. Why did they abandon this site?"

"It would seem that according to the tablet," said the foreman, "they could no longer afford the green fees."

30

Ben came into the clubhouse after finishing his round of golf and sat down at a table to chat with a few of the boys.

"How was your game?" one of the guys asked him.

"It was great," said Ben. "I've become quite a good putter."

"You, a good putter?" said one of the other guys. "I kinda find that hard to believe."

"Well you *can* believe it," said Ben, "I only putted twenty-eight times today, and I owe it all to my new glasses."

"Your new glasses?" said another of the men. "What did your new glasses have to do with it?"

"Simple," said Ben. "They're bifocals. When I look through them, there are two balls—one big and one small. When I look at the hole, there are two holes—one big and one small. All I do now is knock the small ball into the big hole!"

31

The golfer must have missed one putt too many, because he threw down his putter, dropped to his knees, and raised his arms to the sky.

"Jesus, I can't take it any more," he screamed to the heavens. "I defy you to come down here and fight fair. Bring your Father, I don't care. I'll even let you play your best ball!"

32

"You know, I've been a member here for months," the man complained to the head pro, "and in that whole time, no one has spoken to me. Maybe you would be able to suggest a way for me to meet some new people?"

"That's an easy one," said the pro. "If you want to meet people fast, next time you're out on the course, try picking up the wrong ball."

33

Two women who hadn't seen each other in a while ran in to each other in the parking lot of their golf club the other morning.

"So what's new?" asked the first woman.

"I just got a brand-new set of clubs for my husband," the second woman said.

"Sounds like you got a pretty good deal," said the first.

34

Todd had been very unhappy with his golf game as of late. It hurt his wife to see him this way, knowing how much he loved the game. One morning, before he headed to the course, she called him into the kitchen.

"I know your game's been frustrating you, dear," she said, "but I want you to try and enjoy yourself more. From now on when you go out to play, I want you to look only at the positive side of your game. No more negatives. Do you understand me?"

"Yes, ma'am, I understand," he said, and off he went.

Later that afternoon, Todd returned from the course and walked in the house with a big smile on his face.

"Hey, you're smiling," said his wife. "I see you've taken my advice."

"That's right," said Todd. "You're looking at Mr. Positive Golfer from now on."

"So how did you play?" she asked.

"I played great," he said. "I played so great that on the par three seventeenth hole I came *that close* to getting a hole-in-one."

"A hole-in-one! Why that's wonderful!" replied his wife. "How much did you miss it by?"

"Four strokes."

35

Palmer and Gary made plans to play a round of golf one afternoon. They got to the first tee, and Palmer realized that he didn't have any golf balls.

"I'm such a yodel," said Palmer. "But not to worry. I'll just play with an imaginary ball. It'll be fine."

And off they went.

Through seventeen holes, Palmer had managed to hold onto a one-shot lead. (Big surprise.) They came to the eighteenth tee and Gary had had enough.

"I'm playing the eighteenth hole with my own imaginary ball," he said, and proceeded to tee up nothing and take a powerful swing.

"Oh boy," he said, "look at that baby fly—280 yards smack down the middle of the fairway."

He lifted his tee out of the ground and walked over to where Palmer was standing. "You're up," he said.

Palmer walked over, teed up his nothing, and took a long, hard swing.

"Alright!" he exclaimed. "Two hundred seventy-five yards straight down the pike, just by your ball." He picked up his tee, and they headed down the fairway together.

They arrived at their tee shots, and Palmer, finding himself with 150 yards to the flag, pulled out a seven iron and took his cut.

"It's up in the air," he said. "It's a beautiful, high arcing shot, flying right toward the hole. It's bouncing just over the flag. The spin is catching. It's rolling back at the cup. Oh my God, it's in the cup for an eagle! I win the match! I win the match!"

"Not so fast, dummy," said Gary. "It looks like you're disqualified."

"It looks like I'm disqualified?" shouted Palmer. "How can I possibly be disqualified?"

"Seems you weren't paying attention," said Gary. "You played my ball!"

36

It was the first weekend in November, and Davey and Bob got together for a round of golf.

"So how was your Halloween?" Davey asked.

"It was actually pretty neat," said Bob. "Our entire village got together and decorated the town with all kinds of spooks and goblins in an effort to scare as many people as possible."

"That's nothing," said Davey. "You wanna talk about scaring lots of people. One of my friends filmed my golf swing, and we projected it up onto the clouds on Halloween night. We heard there were reports of people freaking out in three counties!"

37

Mark and Craig were in the middle of playing a round of golf one afternoon, when they happened to catch up to two women playing ahead of them. The women were playing quite a bit more slowly than the men would have liked, so Mark decided he was going to walk ahead and catch up to them and ask if they would mind if he and Craig played through. He takes off down the fairway and gets about three quarters of the way to where the women are when he suddenly drops his head. He turns around and walks briskly back to where his friend Craig is standing and waiting for him with a puzzled look on his face.

"What happened?" Craig asked. "Why did you turn around and hightail it back like that?"

"Oh boy," Mark said. "That was too close for comfort. Just as I almost got to them, I realized one of those women was my wife...and the other one was my girlfriend."

"Don't worry about it," said Craig with a little chuckle, "I'll take care of it."

And with that he headed off down the fairway toward the two women. But wouldn't you know it, just as he got close to them, he too suddenly dropped his head, turned around, and hustled on back to where Mark was standing.

"What in the world made you do that?" asked Mark.

"Small world," whispered Craig.

38

Jesus and St. Patrick were out on the back nine one day when the skys began to darken, and a thunderstorm came blowing in. Suddenly the thunder began to roar, and the lightning began to crack. Jesus turned quickly to St. Patrick.

"This storm looks dangerous," he said. "We'd better get in before one of us gets hit by the lightning."

"There's nothing to worry about," said St. Patrick, casually going over to his bag and pulling out an iron. "Just stay close to me," he said, and he headed off down the fairway holding the iron up over his head.

"Are you crazy?" cried Jesus. "You'll be killed."

"Nonsense," said St. Patrick. "This is a one iron. Not even your Father can hit a one iron!"

39

Charlie passed away. In his will, one of his requests was to be buried on the green of his beloved fourteenth hole at his home golf course. The fourteenth hole at his club was a very long par three with a huge bunker in front of a very small green. In all the years Charlie was a member of the club, he never so much as once managed to hit that green in regulation. He always ended up in the bunker. Now it was his wish to spend all eternity on that green.

Charlie's wife met with the board of governors of the club and they informed her that, unfortunately, they could not permit her to bury Charlie on the green. Perhaps, they suggested, she might consider having Charlie cremated and sprinkling his ashes on the green instead. This sounded fair to Charlie's wife and she agreed.

Several days later all of Charlie's golfing buddies got together on the fourteenth green at sunset and held a brief, but moving, ceremony at the conclusion of which, Charlie's wife opened the urn and began to pour out the ashes.

Suddenly, from out of nowhere, a big gust of wind came blowing over from the back of the green...and blew the ashes into the trap.

40

The new golfer was eager to show off his game to one of the better players at the club he had just joined, so he invited the fellow out to play a round. When they had finished, the newbee turned to his guest.

"I just want you to know that it was so important to me that I improve my game that I spent over fifteen thousand dollars on lessons," he said. "What do you think?"

"I think you'll want to meet my brother-in-law," he replied.

"Why, is he a golfer also?" the newbee asked.

"No," said the man, "he's a consumer frauds attorney."

41

The golfer was complaining to his nagging wife.

"Why can't you ever just shut up," he said. "You're going to drive me out of my mind!"

"Wouldn't be much of a drive," she said. "More like a blown two-inch putt."

42

"I played golf with our club pro last Tuesday," Jim was bragging to his friends at work, "and after eighteen holes, would you believe, there was only a one-point difference in our scores?"

"No, we wouldn't" said his friends. "What did the pro shoot?"

"He shot a seventy," Jim said.

"And what did you shoot?" they asked him.

"I shot a *one*-seventy," said Jim.

43

The hacker came upon a hole that, as its claim to fame, was said to possess the world's largest fairway bunker. Naturally, his tee shot, as if drawn by a magnet, found its way right into the heart of this monster. As they reached the abyss, the hacker peered over the edge and turned to his caddie.

"What club do you suggest?" he asked him.

"It really doesn't much matter, sir," was the caddie's response, "but may I suggest that you don't go in there without an adequate supply of food and water."

44

It was the talk of the local club.

"Did you hear what happened to Jon?" asked one of the men in his regular foursome.

"No, I didn't," said another of the members.

"He was in Hawaii on a golfing trip, and he almost drowned," said his friend.

"Almost drowned," said the other member. "That's terrible. How did that happen?"

"It seems he had been saving for this trip for a long time, and all he wanted to do was to play one decent round of golf while he was there. Evidently he played up to his usual lousy standard, because the way I heard it, after slicing one too many tee shots over a cliff and into the ocean, he couldn't take it anymore and he just lost it. He took his bag with all the clubs in it and threw the whole shooting match over the cliff and into the sea."

"So how did he almost drown?" asked the member.

"He almost drowned," said his friend, "when he dove in after them."

45

"Have you noticed the way that new member behaves?" The gossips at the club were discussing in their usual after-golf gabfest.

"It's shameless," said one.

"Totally unacceptable," said another.

"Absolutely reprehensible," said a third.

"What in the world are you all carrying on about?" asked a late arrival to the discussion.

"We're talking about that new member," they said. "He needs to see a psychiatrist."

"What makes you say that?" asked the latecomer.

"The man must be a nut case," they said. "He treats golf as if it were a *game!*"

46

Jack came into the clubhouse one Sunday afternoon sporting a big black eye.

"What happened to you?" asked one of his friends.

"Have you noticed that beautiful young woman who just joined the club?" Jack asked.

"Sure," said his friend. "Who hasn't?"

"I happened to be standing by the first tee when she came over and took the cover off her clubs."

"So?" said his friend.

"I told her it looked like she had a really nice set."

47

A group showed up at the course for their usual game and were quite surprised to find the parking lot entrance totally blocked off.

"What seems to be the problem?" they asked the attendant manning the barricade.

"The course is closed until further notice," he said.

"Closed until further notice?" they said with more than a little shock and dismay. "Why on earth would they do that?"

"It's the Sunday golfers," said the attendant. "Seems they discovered the ruins of an ancient city that had been buried under the course a thousand years ago."

48

First golfer: "How was your game today?"

Second golfer: "It was horrible."

First golfer: "C'mon, how horrible could it have been?"

Second golfer: "It was so bad I lost three balls in the washers!"

49

Sally called Susan the other afternoon in tears.

"He's left me, he's left me," Sally sobbed over the phone.

"What are you getting so upset about?" said Susan. "The worthless bum has left you countless times before, and every time he's come crawling back, so what's the big deal?"

"This time's different," cried Sally. "He's left me for good. He took his golf clubs!"

50

"One thing I've noticed about golf," one fellow said to another.

"What's that?" said the other.

"Golf is the only game where the ball may not lie well, but the players sure do."

51

"So how did your game go today?" the wife asked her husband.

"Great," he said. "I shot three under on the eighteenth hole."

"Three under on the eighteenth hole!" she exclaimed. "Even I know the eighteenth hole is a 425-yard par four. How could you possible have been three under?"

"Easy," he said, "I was one under a tree, two under my cart and three under the clubhouse."

52

Tom came into the clubhouse with his head so low it was practically dragging on the ground.

"Bad round, Tom?" one of his friends asked as he came into the lounge.

"Bad doesn't describe it," said Tom. "It was so brutal that if it had been a prize fight, they would have stopped it after twelve holes."

53

"I get a little bit annoyed at how incredibly cheap some of the members are at this club," a man complained to his friend one day.

"Why do you say that?" his friend asked.

"It's one thing to pick up lost balls," he groused, "but heck, the least they could do is to wait until they stop rolling."

54

The golf pro took the novice woman player out to the practice range for her first lesson.

"The first thing you need to do," the pro said, taking a golf ball out of his pocket and holding it up to her, "is tee the ball."

"Listen, Bub," she snapped. "Let's get one thing straight from the get-go. Just because I'm a woman *and* I'm new to the game, there's no need for you to be condescending, so let's just cut the baby talk right now."

55

The condemned golfer was sentenced to hang at high noon for his crimes. (He was guilty of more than just having an ugly slice.) As he approached the platform where the noose was to be placed around his neck, the executioner asked him, "Do you have any last requests?"

"Yes, as a matter of fact, I do," said the man. "How about a couple of practice swings?"

56

"What are you doing out here on a Sunday morning?" the boys asked Paul, when he showed up at the course. "We figured you'd be in church today."

"Well," said Paul, "it was a toss-up whether I'd play golf or go to church...and I had to toss up twelve times."

57

Four guys teed off one afternoon and almost immediately found themselves behind another foursome. Now this is no big thrill under normal circumstances, but this was not just any other foursome they found themselves behind. These lucky guys found themselves playing behind possibly the worst four players to have ever picked up a set of sticks. These guys were horrid. Their shots would go in every which direction. When they finally did somehow manage to get onto a green, they seemed to putt everywhere except at the hole. It was the worst display anyone had ever seen, and these guys were stuck behind them. Needless to say, they were not happy campers.

When they were finally able to finish the round, they decided to go have a drink in the bar and cool off—their tempers, that is. And as they walked into the bar, who do you think they saw sitting at a table having a meal? You guessed it, the foursome that had ruined their day. They were ready to go over to the table and start a riot but decided it wouldn't be prudent, so instead, they called over the club manager to complain.

"You've got to do something about those guys over there," they said to the manager as he came over. "They're the worst players ever to pick up a set of golf clubs. They absolutely ruined our entire day, and we want you to do something about it."

"I'm terribly sorry, gentlemen," said the manager, "but it's really not their fault they play like they do. You see all four of those men are blind, so we must try to be a little understanding of their situation."

"Understanding you say," said one of the men. "All I understand is if that's their situation, fine—let them play at night!"

58

In order to help promote the game of golf in his area, a pro at one of the local clubs took a booth at a nearby mall where he would be able to offer lessons to a wide group of people.

As he was sitting in his booth one afternoon, a woman, who as it happens had taken her first lesson the day before, stopped by with a friend of hers.

"Hello," said the pro to the two women, "are you here for a lesson today?"

"Oh no," said the woman. "I brought my friend to learn today. Don't you remember? You taught *me* how to play *yesterday*."

59

A hacker went out to the course one day to play a round of golf and found himself paired with a priest. As they worked their way around the front nine, he couldn't help but notice that before every shot, the priest would get down on one knee and pray to the Lord. After playing a particularly brutal front nine, the hacker turned to the priest and asked, "Father, may I ask you a question?"

"Of course, my son," said the priest. "What would you like to know?"

"I've noticed that before every shot, you stop and kneel down and pray. Is there any particular reason you do that?"

"Of course there is, my son," explained the priest. "I pray before every shot so that I can count on the Lord's assistance to help my ball fly straight and true."

"Wow, sounds like a great idea," said the hacker. "Do you think it would work for me?"

"No way, my son," said the priest, much to the hacker's amazement.

"What do you mean, no way?" he said. "Why wouldn't it work for me?"

"Because, my son," said the priest, "you're such a lousy player!"

60

A very unhappy fellow was sitting alone at a bar one evening feeling sorry for himself. His marriage was not going well, and he was contemplating having an extramarital affair. As he was mulling this over, it seemed he was thinking out loud.

"How in the world did I get myself into this," he said. "It's just too damn much trouble. It's always worse than expected, there's no pleasure in it at all, it's expensive, the whole thing has my wife crazy, and there's no hope that things will get any better."

"Pardon me, friend," interrupted the man sitting next to him at the bar, "but I couldn't help overhearing you. If you don't mind my saying so, what did you expect when you took up golf!"

61

After another frustrating day out on the links, Harold was once again sitting at the dinner table bemoaning his lack of playing ability.

"If only I had John Daly's length," he complained.

"I know," moaned his wife, who was by now becoming so sick at having to listen to his carrying on day after day that she couldn't sit quietly and take it anymore. "If you only had John Daly's length, if you only had John Daly's length. Let me tell you something, Buster, the only thing that having John Daly's length would mean to your game is that you'd be able to hit the ball that much farther into the woods!"

Arriving late at his club one Sunday morning, George found himself in the position of having to take the last caddie available. This, as usual, was a crusty old veteran named Tom whom everyone at the club called... Crusty Old Tom. Anyway, the reason Crusty Old Tom was always the last caddie available was that he was getting on in years and tended to be a little on the difficult side. Having been involved with the game for most of his life, he had all the answers and Lord help any "namby, pamby" (his words, not mine) weekend golfer who thought he knew better.

So off they went, and by the time they reached the eighteenth hole George was beside himself. He felt bad for the old guy, but the fact remained that Crusty Old Tom was doing a number on his game. No matter what the situation, Tom would never give George enough club for the shot at hand. George, to his credit, tried everything he could think of to finagle out of using it when Crusty Old Tom gave him the wrong club. Crusty Old Tom, bless him, would have none of it, insisting that George use only the club *he* selected and he went so far as to question George's intellect and, once or twice, even his parentage when George would be foolish enough to question his choice.

After what seemed like the longest round of all time (at

least to George), they finally arrived at the par four eighteenth. George hit a lovely drive down the center of the fairway leaving himself about 210 years to the flag. When they arrived at his ball, Crusty Old Tom handed George a five iron. Fully determined that he was going to have at least one decent hole, George took the five iron in hand and calmly walked back over to his bag and replaced it. Much to Crusty Old Tom's chagrin, George pulled out his three iron and headed back to his ball. As he walked past Crusty Old Tom, George heard him say, "Too much club, Mister."

George didn't want to hear it. He swung that three iron like a man in the Zone. The ball rose from the fairway and headed as if on a clothesline directly at the hole. The ball took one big bounce in front of the green and proceeded to roll right at the cup. When they arrived at the green, they found, much to George's delight and amazement, that the ball had actually rimmed the cup and stopped all of one-half inch behind the hole! George was understandably excited and let out a yip to which Crusty Old Tom responded with a disapproving shake of his head.

"Why in the world are you shaking you head like that?" asked George.

Crusty Old Tom just handed him his putter and said, "Sir, I *told* you it was too much club."

63

Aging Golfer to Doctor: "Doc, ya gotta help me live to be 120 years old."

Doctor to Aging Golfer: "Why do you have to live to be 120?"

Aging Golfer to Doctor: "I want to shoot my age!"

64

This was getting strange even for a guy who was a little strange to begin with. Since he had taken up golf, every night before Herman would go to sleep he had gotten in a strange practice. He would kneel down by the side of his bed, clasp his hands together, look up to the heavens and say this prayer:

"Oh, Lord," he would begin, "please use your almighty powers to watch over my dear friend and golfing buddy Murray. Please see that no harm ever befalls him and that he lives a long and healthy life."

After quietly enduring several months of this ritual, his wife couldn't take it anymore. She had to ask.

"I don't get it," she said to Herman after he finished his little prayer. "I appreciate your feelings for your friend Murray, but isn't this almost nightly business of praying for him getting a little silly. I don't hear you offering any prayers for me."

"That's completely different," said Herman.

"And why is it completely different?" asked his wife.

"For one simple reason," Herman said. "If anything ever happened to you, it wouldn't make me the worst golfer at the club!"

65

A fellow from back East took a golfing holiday to Arizona. Upon arriving at a course outside of Scotsdale the first morning, he was disappointed to learn that all the caddies at the course were tied up for a tournament that day. The head pro apologized profusely and asked whether the man might not be interested in possibly using a donkey they had at the course for just such a situation, for no fee, of course. The man figured why not, and his clubs were loaded onto the donkey and they headed toward the first tee.

"Oh, by the way," the pro said as they headed out. "There is one thing you need to know about this donkey. For some reason, he likes to sit on golf balls. He'll always find your ball, but he may, from time to time, plop himself down on one. Not to worry. In the event he should do this, simply reach under him and pull the ball out. He'll get up and continue on."

That being said, they headed out onto the course, and for a

while everything was just fine. Two or three times the fellow had to reach under the donkey and pull out his ball, but it was no big deal because just as the pro said, after he'd remove the ball, the donkey would get right up and continue on. And besides, this was a target golf course and the donkey *was* doing a good job of finding his errant shots. Then, however, the trouble began. They reached the twelfth hole which was a long par four where the tee shot was blind over a hill. The fellow sliced his tee shot and stood there as the donkey galloped over the hill after it. When he climbed over the hill, he saw the donkey sitting up to it's chest in a water hazard. He went over the hazard, stripped down to his skivvies, and dove in. He took a deep breath and dived under the donkey. No ball. He came up for air and tried again. No ball. After two more attempts, he was about ready to drown. He tried pushing the donkey. He tried pulling on its bridle. No go. He couldn't get this donkey to move no matter how he tried. He finally got fed up and grabbed his clothes and stormed back to the clubhouse.

"What are you trying to do to me?" he yelled at the pro. "I don't mind having to get my ball out from under this damn donkey every now and again, but now he's sitting out in the middle of this lake with my clubs on his back and for the life of me, I can't get him to budge!"

"Oh my, sir," exclaimed the pro, "I'm so sorry. I should have told you."

"Should have told me what?" coughed the man.

"It seems," said the pro, "that the donkey also likes to sit on the occasional fish."

66

An American tourist was overseas playing golf at a course in Ireland, and it seems he was having his usual lousy time of it. On one hole he hit the ball so far into the woods he was sure he would get lost trying to find it, but in he went anyway. After a while, he finally gave up the search. By now he was so upset, he just sat down on a rock and in his misery called out, "I wish I could be the world's best golfer. I'd give anything to make it happen."

Suddenly, he heard a giggle from behind him. He must have jumped five feet off that rock and whirled around to come face to face (more like knee to face) with a real, live leprechaun. After getting over the initial shock of what he was seeing, he asked the leprechaun what he was doing there.

"Why, sir," said the little fellow, "you called for me."

"I called for you?" the man asked incredulously.

"Sure you did," replied the leprechaun. "You just made a wish and now I'm here to fulfill that wish for you."

"You mean you have the power to make me the greatest golfer in the whole world?" the man asked.

"That I do," replied the leprechaun, "but like anything else in life, there is a price that must be paid."

"Anything, anything," said the man. "I don't care what it takes. By the way," he paused, "what *does* it take?"

"The cost is very high," said the leprechaun. "You will become impotent!"

The man turned away and thought about it for a moment. He then turned back to the leprechaun and said, "Fine. This is what I want, and if that's the price that I have to pay, then so be it."

With a tap of his cane, the Earth shook and the leprechaun said, "It is done. Return home and begin entering competitions."

"Thank you, thank you," the man said, as he ran from the woods, wanting to get back to the United States as soon as possible.

"Dunna you be athanking me so fast," said the leprechaun with a sly chuckle that the man never heard.

Upon his return home, the man realized the leprechaun was good to his word. He began entering competitions and he won every one. Within a year, he found himself the winner of all four majors and was considered far and away the best player in the world. The best ever.

One morning he was alone in the locker room after giving an exhibition at a local club. He opened his locker and was quite surprised to find the leprechaun standing inside.

"What in the world are you doing here?" he asked.

"Just wanted to check on how things were going," said the leprechaun with a nasty little smirk. "Now that you've gotten what you wanted, I was curious as to whether or not it was worth the price?"

"Actually," said the man, much to the leprechaun's dismay, "what with my being the priest of a rather small parish, it hasn't been much of an inconvenience at all."

67

Young Zach had been working at his new caddying job for three days when he arrived home early in the afternoon.

"What brings you home so early in the day?" his mother asked, as he walked in the door.

"I got fired" he mumbled, as he walked past her and into his room.

"You got fired?" she said, following him into the room. "How did you get yourself fired after only three days? Were you late getting there?"

"No, I wasn't late," he said.

"Did you not get along with someone?"

"No," he replied, "I got along fine with everybody."

"Then I don't understand," said his mother. "Why did you get fired?"

"I'm sorry, Mom," Zach said, "but no matter how hard I tried, I just couldn't keep myself from laughing."

68

The cheap, old skinflint met his caddie (with whom he was not at all pleased at having to employ to begin with) up by the first tee. The caddie placed his bag down and handed him his driver.

"Before we head out," cracked the old guy, "I want to know something. How good are you at finding lost balls?"

"As it happens, sir," said the caddie, "I take great pride in my ability to find lost balls."

"So then what are you just standing around for?" snapped the old guy. "Get out there and find one so we can get going!"

A fellow teed off on the par four eighth hole at his club one day and sliced the ball off into the woods. As he went in to retrieve it, a genie suddenly popped out from behind a tree and stood right in front of him.

"I am the genie of the forest," he said, "and you are my new master. I am prepared to offer you three wishes."

"You are...you will..." stuttered the obviously startled but intrigued man.

"Yes," said the genie, "but there is one thing you must do first before I can grant you your three wishes."

"What is it?" asked the man, who was now getting caught up in the whole idea. "I'll do anything you ask."

"To get your three wishes, you must agree to let me spend the night with your wife."

"Spend the night with my wife!" exclaimed the man. "How can you expect me to let you spend the night with my wife?"

"If you want your three wishes," said the genie, "this is what you must do."

The man thought about it for a few moments and finally, deciding that three wishes were certainly better than none, agreed.

"It is done," said the genie. "Leave me now. Go call your wife, and tell her to expect me. You must not for any reason return home until tomorrow morning."

The man did as he was told. He called his wife, told her what was going to happen, and did not return home until the next morning.

As he arrived home the next morning and walked up to the front door, it opened from the inside and out came the genie, who proceeded to walk right past him.

"Hey! Where are you going?" he yelled to the genie. "What about my three wishes?"

"Are you kidding?" he laughed. "You still believe in genies?"

70

The exmajor-league baseball player was sitting in the bar with some friends after his first time out on the golf course, nursing both a drink and his ego.

"It's absolutely unbelievable," he griped.

"What's unbelievable?" one of his friends asked.

"What's unbelievable is that I played major league ball for twenty years and it took me that long to get two thousand hits."

"Yeah," his friend asked, "so what's your point?"

"My point," he said, "is that I managed to get the same number of hits my very first time out on a golf course."

71

Two friends were driving to the golf course one morning when one of them decided to wax philosophical.

"You know, I was thinking," he said to his friend. "Golf is a lot like taxes."

"Okay," replied his friend, "I'll bite. Why is golf like taxes?"

"Simple," said his friend, "You spend your whole life driving your heart out for the green, and, no matter what happens, you always end up in a hole."

72

A few of the fellows were sitting around the locker room commiserating after having played a particularly awful round of golf.

"You all think you played terribly," said the last guy to come in from the course. "Let me tell you what bad golf is. I played so badly that all I have to say is that it's a good thing I'm not a farmer."

"I don't get it," said one of the other guys. "Why is it a good thing you're not a farmer?"

"Because," said the first guy, "if I was a farmer, everything I'd grow would come up sliced!"

73

The mark of a good caddie is that no matter how bad the situation, a good caddie will always have something positive to say to his charge. I remember just such a time when I came upon the fourteenth tee at my local course. Things were a little backed up that day, and the group in front of my foursome was about to tee off. One gentleman addressed his ball, took a mighty swing, but, unfortunately, came nowhere close to hitting it. What could have been an ugly moment was saved by his caddie, who immediately walked over the man and said, "It would have been a beautiful shot if you hadn't missed the ball, sir, but it was a wonderful swing nonetheless."

74

"So how did the day go?" his wife asked, as he came through the door from his day out on the links.

"Well, for what it's worth, I hit the woods great," he said.

"Why that's wonderful, sweetheart," she said.

"Yeah," he replied sarcastically, "now all I have to do is learn how to hit out of them!"

Two fellows came together on the way to the locker room after their rounds of golf and got into a conversation.

"So how did you play today?" the first man asked.

"All things considered," said the second fellow, "I can't complain. Besides, who would listen? How did you do?"

"Actually, I played pretty badly," said the first man, "but at least I did manage to birdie the par sixteen eighteenth hole, so the day wasn't a total loss."

"Well, good for you," said the second fellow before it dawned on him. "Hey, wait a minute," he said, "There's no such thing as a par sixteen hole."

"Seeing as I happen to own the course," came the response, "there is now!"

Ed came into the house wearing the longest face his wife had ever seen.

"I'm sorry, sweetheart," she said. "Bad day at the course?"

"Bad doesn't describe it," he said.

"How bad was it?" she asked.

"It was so bad," he said, "that at one point during the round, one of the guys from the foursome behind us came over and asked me if my husband played."

77

Two friends were sitting in the clubhouse discussing equipment when the subject of woods came up.

"In my opinion," said the first guy, "the best wood in my bag is my five wood. It's gotten me out of trouble more times than I can remember."

"I have to disagree with you," said his friend. "The best wood in *my* bag has gotten me out of more trouble than all the five woods on the planet *ever* could."

"What wood is that?" the first guy asked.

"My pencil!"

78

The bartender was setting up for the day in the grillroom overlooking the eighteenth green. Suddenly, a golf ball came crashing through one of the windows. About two minutes later, a gentleman who had just joined the club came through the patio door with a puzzled look on his face.

"Excuse me," he said to the bartender, "may I ask you a question?"

"Why certainly, sir," replied the bartender. "What would you like to know?"

"Perhaps you can tell me," he asked, "is this room considered out of bounds?"

79

The women were in the kitchen listening to the men going on and on in the next room, talking about nothing but golf and sex.

"You know," said one of the ladies, "it's amazing how at their ages they can spend so much time talking about golf and sex."

"What's so amazing about it?" said another. "...at their ages, about all they can *do* is talk about it."

80

Two women meet outside the supermarket.
"How's your husband's golf game?"

"It's interesting"

"Interesting? How so?"

"Seems the older he gets, the better he used to be."

81

As they were heading to the course one morning, two older fellows were bemoaning their fading skills.

"It's really so very sad," said the first man. "It wasn't too long ago that I could walk up to that tee, pull my trusty driver out of my bag, and just airmail that ball outta there."

"Yeah," said his buddy, "I know just what you mean. I gave up thinking about airmailing balls a long time ago. At this point, I'm happy if I can just manage to parcel post it to the right zipcode."

82

Two men were paired together one day at a resort course in the Caribbean. One of the men was in his eighties, and the other was in his twenties. After they had played several holes, the younger man noticed that the older man had an interesting habit of walking right up to the ball and striking away at it without so much as the least bit of preparation or preshot routine.

"If you don't mind my saying," said the younger man, "I've noticed you don't take a practice swing before hitting the ball. I admire that you can just get there and hit it like that."

"Don't be too impressed," said the older man. "I'd love to take practice swings, but what you have to realize is that at my age, I have no swings to waste."

83

A foursome was out on the course about midway through their round when they looked up to the sky and saw the storm clouds gathering in the west. Where the smart thing to do would, of course, be to call it quits for the day, these geniuses decide they can continue to play. All they have to do is to stay ahead of the storm. They finished the hole they were on as they heard the thunder in the distance. As they played the next hole, the storm was getting closer. As they played the hole after that, the storm was moving in closer. They got to the next tee, and as the first guy was about to hit, the storm closed in. There was a huge clap of thunder, and from out of the heavens a lightning bolt pierced the sky and crashed into the fairway no more than fifty feet in front of him.

"That's it. I don't care what you guys say," he said, grabbing his bag and heading for the clubhouse. "As far as I'm concerned, when God says he wants to play through, He plays through."

84

It was a beautiful morning out on the golf course. The Smith foursome teed off at 7:05 and headed off down the first fairway. Suddenly, from out of nowhere, a huge black cloud appeared on the course directly over the foursome. Before they had any chance to react, four bolts of lightning came crashing to the ground, killing all four men right where they stood.

Next thing they knew, the four of them were standing at the entrance to Heaven before the Pearly Gates. The gatekeeper looked at his book as they approached and said, "Ah, the O'Brian foursome, right on time. Welcome."

"Um, excuse me, sir," said one of the men, "but we're not the O'Brian foursome, we're the Smith foursome."

"The Smith foursome!" exclaimed the gatekeeper, rechecking his book. "That's impossible. You teed off at 7:05. You must be the O'Brian foursome."

"Sorry to disappoint," said another of the men, "but we are the Smith foursome. The O'Brian foursome showed up late this morning, and we took their 7:05 tee-off time. They teed off directly behind us."

"Oh my," replied the now clearly upset gatekeeper, "this will never do. It's just not your time. I'm going to have to send you back."

"Send us back?" the men said. "How can you send us back? We're dead. You can't send us back now. How in the world are we going to explain that little trick? It's going to be very inconvenient, to say the least."

"I have no choice but to send you back," said the gatekeeper, "but I'll tell you what I'll do. Because of what you've been through, I will grant one wish among the four of you. Just tell me what you want."

The four guys huddled together for a few moments and then turned to the gatekeeper.

"Have you decided upon your wish?" he asked.

"Yes, we have," they said. "We'd like to go back as transvestites."

"You want to go back as transvestites?" asked the stunned gatekeeper. "Why in the world do you want to go back as transvestites?"

"Simple," they said. "That way we could play from the red tees and still fool around with women!"

A group of people were sitting around the grillroom one afternoon watching the later players tee off on the first hole. In one of the groups, a man set his ball on the tee and proceeded to hit what could have been the mother of all slices. Now, under normal circumstances, this would have gone down in the books as just another lousy tee shot; however, on this particular course the first hole ran parallel to a busy street. What happened is that this guy's tee shot flew over the club fence and crashed into the windshield of a passing school bus loaded with children. The driver of the bus, taken quite by surprise, lost control of the wheel causing the bus to plow into several cars on the road forcing some of them up onto the crowded sidewalk sending people scattering in every which direction before it crashed into a group of storefronts. The people in the grillroom who had witnessed this whole fiasco stood in shock as the fellow who hit the ball calmly picked up his tee and proceeded down the first fairway as if absolutely nothing at all had happened.

Needless to say, there was quite a crowd waiting for this fellow as he came down the eighteenth fairway back towards the clubhouse. Just as the crowd began to head for the door, probably to massacre this guy, the head pro jumped up in front of the group.

"Ladies and gentleman," he said, "being the head pro at this club, it is my responsibility to handle this situation and that is exactly what I intend to do. Now all of you just remain here, and I will take care of things."

So out he went to the eighteenth green and waited for the man. When the man arrived, the pro took him off to the side and informed him of what had happened. Upon hearing the story, the poor fellow felt horrible.

"Dear God, this is terrible," he said to the pro. "What in the world can I do about it?"

"Well," said the Pro, "The *first* thing you need to do, is strengthen your grip."

86

Bill was having a really bad day on the golf course. Right around the fourteenth hole it seems he had missed one putt too many. He let loose with a fairly impressive string of profanities, grabbed his putter, and stormed of toward the lake by the fifteenth tee.

"Uh, oh," said his caddie to one of his playing partners, "There goes *that* club."

"You think so?" said his partner. "I've got five bucks says he misses the water!"

87

Two friends who hadn't seen each other in a while ran into each other at the local golf course.

"Hey," said the first friend, "You look terrific. Have you lost weight?"

"Why thank you for noticing," said the second friend. "I have. I've been on that new golf diet. Perhaps you've heard about it?"

"No, as a matter of fact I haven't," said the first friend. "How does it work?"

"It's really simple," said the second friend. "You live on greens!"

88

"I can't stand playing at my local muni any more," complained Norm. "It's the slowest playing course on the planet."

"What makes you think it's the slowest playing course on the planet?" asked Cliff.

"I'll tell you why," said Norm. "The other day I was looking in my handy dandy golf dictionary and came upon the term slow play. Next to the definition was a picture of my course!"

89

After missing another ridiculously short putt, a jerk of a guy huffed over to his caddie, shoved the putter into his hands and yelled, "You are the world's worst caddie!"

"I'm sorry to disagree, sir," replied the caddie, "but I doubt that I am."

"And what makes you doubt it?" snapped the putz.

"It would be just too much of a coincidence."

90

Sally stopped by Amy's house for an early morning visit. As they sat in the breakfast room having coffee, Amy's husband came walking by on his way out to the golf course.

"My," said Sally, "will you look at him. He's quite a sight. With the fancy outfit, the straw hat, the wingtip shoes, and the expensive clubs, he looks like 'the Shark'."

"He may look like 'the Shark'," chuckled Amy, "but trust me, he plays like 'the Minnow'!"

91

Victor ran over to the fellow he'd just hit with his tee shot. "I'm so sorry," he said to the man. "Are you alright?"

"You could have killed me," said the man, rubbing the spot where the ball hit him.

"I said I was sorry," repeated Victor, "and I did yell 'Fore'. You're supposed to get out of the way."

"Next time try yelling 'Five'," said the man.

"'Five,'" said a puzzled Victor, "What does 'Five' mean?"

"'Five,'" the fellow answered making a fist, "means, '*You're* gonna get hit!'"

92

A man set out for a round of golf with his caddie named Juan. Now, it seems that Juan was quite possibly the worst caddie of all time. He was just awful. All his club selections were wrong and all his yardages were way off. The poor fellow played the worst round of golf of his life. By the eighteenth green he couldn't take it anymore. He pulled a gun out of his golf bag and killed Juan right there on the green. He then proceeded to get into his car and go home. He parked the car in the driveway and walked into the house.

"How did you play?" his wife asked.

"Not very well," he answered, "but things turned out okay."

"How so?" she asked.

"I shot a hole-in-Juan."

Richie was on a business trip to Pakistan. When he found himself with a little free time on his hands, he decided to get in a round of golf. Midway through the front nine, he suddenly developed a horrible toothache. He was rushed to one of the local dentists who proceeded to examine his mouth and, much to his dismay, informed him that not only did he have one bad tooth but he actually had three more teeth that needed immediate work.

"Not so fast," exclaimed Richie. "Before you do anything to me, I would really need to talk to another of your patients about your work."

"Why no problem at all," said the dentist. "It just so happens that about two years ago I performed work on one of your own countrymen. A Mr. Edward Jones from New York City. As I remember it, I filled *five* of his teeth. Perhaps you would like to speak with him?"

"That would be fine," said Richie.

After over an hour of trying, the dentist's nurse was finally able to place the call and get Mr. Jones on the phone.

"Oh yes," said Mr. Jones to Richie, "I remember him well.

You know, it's a funny thing you should call. I was out on the golf course just yesterday when some yutzcup shanked a wormburner off the fifteenth tee and hit me smack in the groin."

"I'm awfully sorry about that," said Richie, "but I'm in quite a bit of pain here myself. If you don't mind my asking, exactly what does that have to do with the dentist's work?"

"Simple," said Mr. Jones. "That was the first time in two years that I forgot how much my teeth hurt!"

94

The pro was having a less than stellar round that day. As if he wasn't having enough trouble with a swing that wouldn't know a groove if it were living in the 60's, he was breaking in a new caddie who hadn't given him anything even resembling the correct yardage for a single shot the entire round. After sailing his tee shot at the par three sixteenth hole thirty yards over the green, he'd had enough. He called over one of the tournament officials.

"I know there's a penalty for throwing a club," he said to the official, "but what I need to know is if there's a penalty for throwing a caddie?"

Three women were playing the ninth hole at their club one sunny Friday. As they approached the green, they noticed a rustling coming from one of the bushes just behind the green. One of the women went over to investigate.

"What was it?" one of the other women asked when she returned.

"You're not going to believe it," she said. "I looked around the side of the bush, and you're not going to believe what I saw. There's a man standing there, going to the bathroom."

"No," gasped the others. "Were you able to see who it was?"

"I don't know. I couldn't tell," she said. "The bushes blocked his face, but from what I did manage to see, the one thing I could tell is that it wasn't my husband."

"Oh, let me go see," said the second woman as she headed over to the bush, returning a few moments later.

"Could you figure out who it is?" her friends asked.

"No. You were right about the bush being in the way," she said. "All I could tell is that from what I saw, it's definitely not my husband either."

"Looks like I'll have to go figure out who this mystery man is," said the third woman, as she too went over to the bush.

"So," they asked upon her return, "were you able to figure out who it is?"

"No," she said, "but I can tell you that not only is it not my husband, but whoever he is, he is definitely *not* a member of this club!"

96

After leaving every putt one roll short of the cup all day long, the frustrated golfer finally asked his playing partners for some advice.

"The first thing you have to do is stop using that Latin American ball," one of them said.

"A Latin American ball?" he asked. "What's a Latin American ball"

"Don't you know?" said his friend. "A Latin American ball is a ball that always needs another revolution."

97

It only seemed like it took forever for the hacker and his group to get around the golf course, his game being what it was. It had actually gotten to the point where laughing at his game had become boring. They finally arrived on the eighteenth tee as the sun was beginning to set. The hacker got up on the tee and managed to hit a shot that actually landed on the fairway.

"They're getting longer," his caddie said to the others.

"See, see, see," the hacker needled his companions. "He said they're getting longer, he said they're getting longer. So there!"

"Actually, sir," said his caddie, as he went past him, "I was referring to the shadows."

98

What do alligators wear when they play golf?
Sportshirts with little middle-aged men on them.

99

A group of four had just reached the eighth green. They're about to putt when all of a sudden a beautiful young woman appears from out of nowhere and begins to run around the green, laughing as she ran. Just as suddenly, two young men appear behind her and start to chase her around the green. The foursome on the green notice that one of the young men is carrying a bucket of sand. After a couple of laps, they manage to

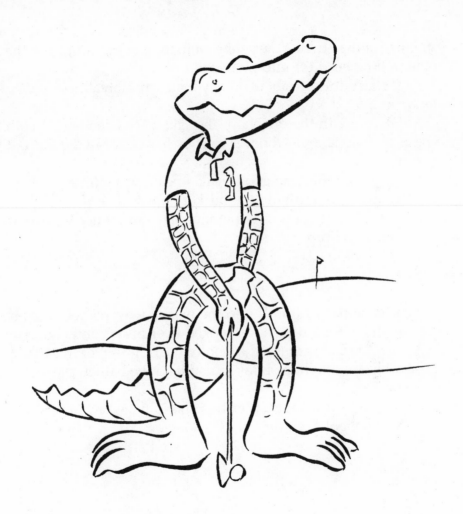

stop one of the guys as the young woman, still laughing, and the other fellow head off into the woods.

"What's this all about?" they asked the breathless young man.

"We work in the pro shop," he said. "My friend and I both chase after Julie and whoever catches her gets to take her out that night."

"That's all well and good," said one of the men, "but what's with your buddy carrying the bucket of sand?"

"Oh, that," said the youngman. "He caught her last week. That's his handicap!"

100

After putting himself into the woods with his tee shot on the par three hole, the hacker looked over his second shot. He had to get the ball through the woods, over a group of trees, past a water hazard and huge bunker, and land the ball on a severely sloped green.

"What do you suggest for this shot?" he asked his caddie.

"How about a prayer book?"

101

Perhaps you heard the story of the professional golfer who was complaining to one of his friends about the terrible season he had that year.

"Aw," said his friend, "how bad could it have been?"

"Are you kidding?" the golfer replied. "My year was so bad that I received a get-well card from the I.R.S."

102

"That's it!" said the exasperated golfer to his insolent young caddie. "I've had enough of your lip. When we get back to the clubhouse, I'm going to report you directly to the caddie master."

"Oooo, I'm so worried," responded the little brat.

"You'd better worry," said the golfer.

"And why should I worry," said the kid. "At the rate you play, by the time we get back, it'll be time for me to retire."

103

A man who thought himself to be a golfer was playing the Sawgrass T.P.C. stadium course in Florida. On one hole he had a rather long approach shot, so he asked his caddie to suggest a club.

"Well," began the caddie, "when I caddied at last week's tournament for Mr. Gary McCord and his ball landed in just about the same spot as yours, he . . . " But before he had a chance to complete his sentence, the impatient player interrupted him.

"Spare me the stories," he said. "Just give me the club McCord used."

"But, sir," the caddie tried to interject.

"But nothing," said the guy. "Just give me the club he used."

"Very well, sir," said the caddie, handing him the club.

The fellow took the club in hand, set up over the ball, and took his swing. They both stood there and watched as the ball flew into the air and came down on the fairway a good thirty yards short of the green.

"Hey," said the fellow wheeling on the caddie, "I wasn't even close to the green."

"Neither was Mr. McCord."

104

It must have been the putt that broke the camel's back because as Paul watched that rotten twelve-incher curl around the lip of the cup and pop out the back, something snapped. You could say he lost it.

"That's it!" Paul screamed. "I can't take it any more. I quit, I quit. I simply WILL NOT play this game ANYMORE! I don't deserve to live anymore."

And with that, he took his putter and proceeded to snap it across his knee like a dried twig. He hurled the pieces off the green and stomped over to his bag, which he grabbed by the strap and dragged towards the lake. When he got to the lake the bag went flying in, followed in rapid succession by each of his shoes. He then stormed off the course and into the locker room where he took out a razor blade and slashed his wrists. Then he took the strap off a bag in the locker room, threw it over one of the shower heads, and hanged himself.

Round about this time, the other three guys in Paul's foursome had finished their round and happened past him hanging there in the shower on their way to the locker room.

"Say, Paul," said one of them in passing, without so much as looking up, "you in for tomorrow?"

"Sure," said Paul, loosening the strap and falling to the floor. "What time?"

105

While there are people who pay attention to detail, some are ridiculous. This one fellow was meticulous to a fault. His caddie hadn't seen anything like it. He finally manages to get to the first green and he's looking at a six-inch putt. You'd have thought he was twenty feet out. He cleans the grass in front of the hole, he wets his index finger and checks the wind, he looks to see where the sun is, and he actually goes so far as to lie down on the ground to check the line. When this is all done, he asks his caddie,

"Were the greens cut this morning?"

"Yes, sir, they were," says the caddie.

"Were they cut from left to right, or from right to left?" he asks.

"Left to right, I believe."

After all that, he finally settles in over the putt, pulls the club back and through, watching as the ball rolls past the hole. Immediately, his head snaps around, and he glares at the caddie.

"What time?"

106

Four women teed off on the par four eleventh hole at their local course. Their tee shots were a little errant, so they were standing in the rough waiting for the group in front of them to clear the green. Suddenly, a ball came flying in from behind, landing between two of the women. They turned around to see two men standing on the tee. They finished their play on the hole and waited by the green for the two men to arrive.

"Hey," said one of the women as the men walked up to the

green, "you should be more careful with those tee shots. You could have hurt somebody."

"I'm terribly sorry," said the guy who almost hit them, "I just didn't have time to yell 'fore'."

"I don't know," grumbled another of the ladies, "You sure seemed to have plenty of time to yell 'DAMN'!"

107

Four men were standing on the twelfth hole about to tee off when, from seemingly out of nowhere, a man came running up to them huffing, puffing, and dragging his clubs behind him.

"Pardon me, gentlemen," he panted, "I just found out my wife is seriously ill and has been rushed to the hospital."

"Is there anything we can do?" they offered.

"If it wouldn't be too much of a bother," he said, "would you mind terribly if I played through?"

108

Charlie bumped into Steve in the locker room at the golf club Wednesday morning.

"Did you hear what happened with Dave?" he asked.

"No," said Steve, "I didn't. What's up?"

"It seems that Dave finished his round earlier than usual on

Sunday. He got changed, went home, walked into his house, and caught his wife in bed with another man."

"You're kidding," said Steve. "What did he do?"

"Lord, I hear it was terrible," said Charlie. "He evidently grabbed the guy, threw him out of the bed onto the floor, pulled out a gun, and shot him dead right there in the bedroom."

"Oh, m-m-my," stammered Steve, who upon hearing the story, proceeded to turn quite pale.

"Say, what's the matter with you?" asked Charlie.

"Whew. Nothing," said Steve, wiping the sweat from his brow. "All I have to say is, thank God he didn't finish early on Saturday."

109

The frustrated hacker blew one shot too many that day. The last was a twelve-inch putt. Evidently needing to vent, he turned to his caddie, as he walked off the green, and said, "You know, you can't caddie."

"Why, that's alright, sir," the caddie replied without breaking stride. "You can't play golf."

110

His wife came home from the practice range.

"How was your lesson, dear?" he asked.

"Great," she said, "I'm not missing the ball by *nearly* as much, anymore."

111

"We've been having big marital problems lately, my wife and I," a fellow confided to his good friend during their golf game. "I don't know who to turn to."

"Have you thought about getting professional help?" offered his friend.

"Yes, of course I have," he said. "But that creates another problem."

"What kind of problem could that create?" his friend asked.

"I can't make up my mind who to go to," he said, "a marriage counselor or my golf pro."

Three friends were paired together with a fourth player for a round of golf. They teed off and everything was proceeding normally until 'round about the fourth hole. It was then that the friends began to notice that this fellow seemed to have a strange little quirk. Every time they would get up to a green, this guy would go into his bag and pull out a huge floppy hat. He'd pull the thing onto his head so it hung almost to his shoulders, walk on the green, and putt out. After putting, he'd roll up the hat and stuff it back into the bag. This same scenario continued on for a few more holes, and one of the men finally had to ask.

"You know," he began, "my friends and I are curious. So far on every hole we've played, each time we've approached a green, you go into your bag and pull out that big old hat, put it on, and then go ahead and putt. Is there any particular reason you do that?"

"Ah, you noticed that," he said. "Well, seeing as you did, I'll let you in on a little secret. You boys may not know it, but you happen to be in the presence of the Lord's worst putter."

"Gee, I'm sorry to hear that," he said. "I guess someone has to be the worst, but what does that have to do with the hat?"

"I'm trying something," he said. "I figure that maybe with the hat, when I walk on the green the Lord won't recognize me."

113

A man was out on the golf course one day, about to tee off on the tenth hole, when he suddenly became ill and collapsed in a delirious heap on the tee. They called 911, and he was rushed to a nearby hospital. In the emergency room he was placed in a bed, and a nurse came by to take his temperature.

"Ninety-nine," she called out, as she looked at the thermometer.

As she said this, the man squirmed in the bed. Five minutes later she came back to take his temperature again.

"One hundred," she called out.

This time when she called out the temperature, the man shuddered. Five minutes later, she returned to take his temperature again.

"One hundred and one," she called out.

With that the poor guy almost jumped out of the bed.

"My God!" he screamed. "What's par at this course?!"

114

Two older fellows were chatting in the locker room after playing a round of golf.

"You know," one said, "the kids of today don't know how to do anything right."

"What makes you say that?" his buddy asked.

"Well, I'll tell ya," he said. "I was out playing with a couple of youngsters just the other day. They couldn't play worth a tinker's damn, and every time they'd screw up a shot, they'd throw their clubs in every which direction."

"Why, that's terrible behavior," said his friend. "I trust you told them, in no uncertain terms, that that type of behavior is totally unacceptable on the golf course."

"Hell no," his friend exclaimed. "What I *did* do, was to tell the little idiots that when you throw a club, at least have the brains to throw it in the direction you have to go!"

115

"So Ed," said Fred, "tell me. How's the old golf game coming along?"

"Not so bad," said Ed. "So far my best score is one twenty-six."

"One twenty-six," said Fred. "That's the best you've been able to do?"

"Hey," said Ed. "You have to take into account that I've only been playing the game for twenty-two years."

116

Three men were standing on the first tee waiting for the fourth who was supposed to play with them. As they stood there, a man came out the clubhouse and staggered his way up to the tee where they were standing. He was totally plastered.

"Lookth like I'll be playin' with you guyth," he managed to spit out, as he pulled his driver out of his bag and began waving it around, over his head.

"Whoa, fella," the other guys said, grabbing him from behind and taking the club out of his hands. "There's no way you are in any condition to drive."

"You're probably right," he hiccupped. "I really shouldn't be driving. Heck, I probably shouldn't even be putting."

117

Two guys met in the parking lot of the golf course and started discussing the day's play.

"So what did you shoot on the first hole?" the first guy asked.

"I got a five," the second guy said.

"Oh," said the first guy. "I got a four. What did you get on the second hole.?"

"I shot a four," said the second guy. "What did you get?"

"I got a three," said the first guy. "What did you get on the third hole?"

"I shot a six," the second guy said. "What did you get?"

"Me? I got a four. What did you get on the fourth hole?" the first guy asked.

"Hey, not so fast," said the second guy. "You first!"

118

A wife couldn't understand her husband's obsession with golf.

"Why do you play so much?" she asked him one morning as he was getting ready to leave for the course. "What is it about that game that has you hooked? It seems like such a waste of time."

"It's not a waste of time at all, dear," he stammered, searching for an answer. "Uh, I play so much golf because, umm, because golf keeps me fit. Yeah, that's it. Golf keeps me fit."

"Golf keeps you fit," she said, looking at him rather skeptically. "Fit for what?"

"Why, it keeps me fit for . . . for . . . for . . . for GOLF!"

119

After hitting his tee shot deep into the woods, the hacker turned to his caddie.

"Did you see where that one went?" he asked.

"No sir, as a matter of fact I didn't," replied the caddie.

"Well, why on earth didn't you watch where it went?" snapped the angry man.

"Frankly, sir," said the caddie, "I was quite unprepared for it to go anywhere."

120

What do golf and sex have in common?

They're two things you can enjoy even if you're lousy at both of them.

121

After many months of fruitless lessons, the golf pro pulled the hacker off to one side.

"Listen," said the pro, "I've always said golf is a game that almost anyone can learn to play. Unfortunately, it looks like you're an almost."

122

Stanley got together with Alan for drinks after golf.

"So, Stan," asked Alan, "how did the tournament go today?"

"It was awful," said Stan. "I never played so badly in my entire life."

"Come on," said Alan. "It couldn't have been that bad."

"Not that bad?" said Stan. "I'll tell you how bad it was. I played so badly that whenever I heard anyone yell 'Fore', I didn't know whether to duck, or if they were just telling me how many people I'd hit."

123

Just as they were about to tee off on the seventeenth hole, one of the men in the foursome suddenly collapsed on the ground, clutching his chest.

"Damn," said his partner, "I don't believe he's having a heart attack."

"What's the matter with you?" said one of the other men. "How could you doubt him. He's turning blue, for God's sake."

"Oh, I don't doubt that the heart attack is real," said his partner, "but this is an important match. I'm just not happy with his timing."

A man named Dumbroski was out with a few friends playing a round of golf one day. His group came to the ninth hole which, at this particular course they were playing, was a long par five where the tee shot had to carry over a rise in the fairway. Dumbroski hit a beautiful tee shot that sailed far down the fairway, disappearing over the rise. As they walked down the fairway and over the rise, Dumbroski was more than a bit surprised to find his ball was nowhere in sight. The only thing in the area where his ball should have been was another golfer crossing the fairway.

"Pardon me," said Dumbroski, "but did you happen to see a ball land right around here?"

"No, as a matter of fact, I don't believe I have," said the man, a little suspiciously.

"If you don't mind my asking, what about that ball in your hand?" asked Dumbroski.

"Oh, that's *my* ball," the man replied.

"Well, my ball had Dumbroski written on it."

"My, now, isn't that a coincidence," said the man, glancing at the ball. "It just so happens that *I'm* playing a Dumbroski."

125

On every hole they played up to that point, this one guy in the foursome was the slowest player anyone had ever seen. He seemed to take forever over the ball, and things were starting to back up on the course because of this clown. Finally, one of the players in the foursome behind them said something to him on the eleventh tee.

"You can complain all you want," said the slowpoke, "but I can address the ball for as long as I feel necessary!"

"Oh yeah," said one of the men in the other foursome, heading towards him. "You won't need to address it. I'm gonna *show* you where it lives!"

126

Bud called his friend in tears.

"I can't believe it," he sobbed. "My wife left me for my golfing partner."

"Get a hold of yourself, man," said his friend. "There are plenty of other women out there."

"Who's talking about her?" said Bud. "He was the only guy I could ever beat!"

127

The aging pro golfer was sitting at breakfast one morning, talking with his wife.

"You know, honey," he said, "I'm worried about retirement."

"What is it you're worried about?" she asked.

"I don't know what I'll do with myself," he said. "Everybody else retires to play golf and fish. That's what I do now!"

128

As the story goes, a Scotsman named Angus played the same golf ball for over twenty-five years. One day, the unthinkable happened. Angus lost his ball. He walked into the golf shop, completely disgusted.

"Well, Seamus," he announced, "here I am agin!"

129

Walter was passing a large, deep bunker on the twelfth hole when he heard cries for help coming from inside it. Looking down into the trap, he saw his friend lying underneath an overturned golf cart, trapped.

"Please, help me," the man called out upon seeing Walter.

"Does our lawyer know you're here?" Walter asked.

"No," groaned the man.

"Great!" said Walter, climbing down into the trap. "Move over."

130

"I can't believe it!" snarled Al, as he walked into the locker room.

"What's the matter?" asked one of his friends.

"The committee fined me for striking my caddie with an eight iron," he said.

"That's too bad," said his friend. "They got you for poor sportsmanship."

"No," said Al, "they fined me for using the wrong club!"

131

Hal had only been playing golf for a few weeks, but he was already driving his friends nuts talking about it—day after day, hour after hour. After one particularly long discussion, one of his friends finally couldn't listen to it anymore.

"Say, Hal," he said, "I know the most difficult thing for *any* new golfer to do. Do *you* know what's the most difficult thing for any new golfer to do?"

"No," said Hal. "What?"

"The most difficult thing for *any* new golfer to do," said his friend, "is to *stop talking about it!*"

132

"It was the most amazing thing that ever happened to me in my life," Jake was telling his friend. "I'm walking down the street Thursday minding my own business when all of a sudden, right in front of me, two men try to abduct this beautiful young woman. I never even had a chance to think. I just reacted and threw myself into them causing a scene, which the two guys obviously had no interest in being a part of, because they took off and ran. The woman immediately broke down in tears as she hugged me and thanked me for saving her.

"Later, when she had a chance to regain her composure she explained to me that she was the daughter of a multimillionaire, and that she wanted to take me to see her father who was sure to reward me for saving her. I told her it wasn't necessary, that I didn't do it for a reward, but she absolutely insisted I take her to see her father. So off we go to see her father in this huge office building with his name over the entrance and everything, and, sure as her word, her father offered me anything I wanted."

"Wow," said his stunned friend, "what did you ask for?"

"I told him that I really wasn't interested in anything, but he was insistent, so I finally told him I liked to play golf and if he really wanted to get me something, why not just get me a golf club."

"A GOLF CLUB!" His friend couldn't believe what he had just heard. "Let me get this straight. You tell me you save a millionaire's beautiful daughter from being kidnapped. She takes you to see her father, who just happens to be one of the richest men in the entire country. The guy offers you anything you want, and all you ask for is a lousy golf club. Are you nuts?"

"Oh, I wouldn't exactly say that," said his friend with a Cheshire grin spreading across his face. "The golf club he bought me...was Pebble Beach!"

133

Doris and Sally ran into each other at the club.

"So I hear you and Harry were recently overseas," Doris said.

"Right you are," said Sally. "We just got back last week. It was a typical Harry trip. He insisted we go to the Holy Land. I had absolutely the worst time of my life."

"I can't believe you had a bad time in the Holy Land," said Doris. "I've been there myself, and I found the Middle East to be the most amazing and exciting place I'd ever been to in my life."

"Who said anything about the Middle East?" asked Sally. "I told you this was one of Harry's trips. We didn't go to the Middle East. We went to St. Andrews."

134

The two old guys walked off the twelfth green and headed for the thirteenth tee.

"So, what did you get?" the first guy asked.

"I got a six," the second guy said.

"A six!" exclaimed the first guy. "You took five just to get out of the bunker."

"Fine," said the second guy, "so make it an eleven."

135

The pro was playing in a tournament and was having a rather bad round. After one particularly errant shot, he slammed his club to the ground and uttered a rather ugly profanity. Immediately, he was face to face with one of the tournament marshals.

"You know, you're not supposed to use profanity on the course," said the marshal. "I'm going to have to fine you one hundred dollars."

"You're going to fine me one hundred dollars for that one little word? You can't be serious," said the pro.

"I sure am," said the marshal.

"Here then," growled the pro, taking five hundred dollars out of his wallet and handing it to the marshal.

"What's this for?" asked the marshal.

"There's a hundred to cover the fine and an extra four hundred to cover what I'm about to say to you!"

136

Tim had a pretty bad day out on the links. It seemed liked every shot he took, he either sliced or pushed the ball. All day, slice or push, push or slice. Even the putts. He was pretty disgusted. When he got home, he threw his clubs in the garage and went into the kitchen where his wife was having a cup of coffee.

"So, how did you play today?" she asked him.
"All right," he said.

137

Tony had what could only be described as a rather strange golf swing. He'd address the ball ("Hello ball!"), take the club half way back, then stop. Then he'd lift the club over his head, then stop. Then he'd finally swing the club through, on occasion, actually hitting the ball. Anyway, one day he was playing with a fellow he'd never met before. This fellow took quite an interest in Tony's swing, never having seen anything like it. After playing a few holes, he felt comfortable enough to ask exactly what type of swing it was.

"Oh," said Tony, "I call it my Pony Express swing."

"Pony Express swing?" said the fellow. "Why do you call it the Pony Express swing?"

"Isn't it obvious?" said Tony. "It's done in three stages!"

138

Jack came skulking into the clubhouse after this round.

"Hey, Jack," his friends asked him when he came into the bar, "how'd you play today?"

"Jack doesn't exist anymore. Don't call me Jack. Jack is dead," he said.

"Why shouldn't we call you Jack anymore?" they asked.

"After all the time I spent in the sand traps today," he said, "I'm officially changing my name to Lawrence!"

139

The hacker met his playing partners on the first tee.

"What's your handicap?" one of the men asked.

"My golf game!"

140

Mike must have had a worse day than usual on the golf course. He came home, got undressed, climbed into bed, and pulled the covers up over his head. His wife came in the room and seeing him like this, tried to pull the covers back down, only to have him yank them up back over his head.

"Oh for God's sake," she said. "What's the matter with you? It's only a golf game. It's not like it's a matter of life and death."

"You're right," came a voice from under the covers. "It's not a matter of life or death. It's *golf.* It's *much* more important than that!"

141

"I don't get it," the new golfer said to his pro after a few lessons. "I thought that golf is supposed to be a rich man's game."

"What is it you don't get?" asked the pro.

"I've been watching all these people play," he said, "and what I don't get, is that if they say golf is supposed to be a rich man's game, then how come all I see are *poor* players?"

142

The minister was paired with a hacker at the local muni one afternoon. After playing a few holes, it became obvious to the minister that this guy was really bad. Not only did his game stink on ice, but with every flubbed shot he would launch into a tirade of obscenities, the likes of which this poor minister had never heard before. Finally after an hour of this guy's ranting and raving, the minister just had to say something.

"Young man," he began. "I want you to know that this type of behavior is completely unnecessary. Why, I played with a man just yesterday who shot a six under par, and not once during the entire round did he so much as raise his voice, much less carry on with every shot the way you do."

"Six under par!" snapped the hacker. "Of course he didn't say anything. *What the Hell* did he have to complain about?!"

143

Old golfers' adage: Give me a set of clubs, a great golf course to play, and a beautiful woman; and you can keep the first two.

144

True golfers' adage: Give me a set of clubs, a great golf course to play, and a beautiful woman; and let's hit the links. She can keep score.

145

"Lee, how'd your round go today?" his friend asked on the way to the parking lot.

"I shot a perfect businessman's score," said Lee.

"What in the world is a perfect businessman's score?" his friend asked.

"A perfect businessman's score is a ninety," said Lee.

"And why is a ninety a perfect businessman's score?" asked his friend.

"Because," said Lee, "anything lower and you'd be neglecting your business, and anything higher and you'd be neglecting your golf game!"

146

Louie and Larry got together for a round of golf at the club. When they met at the first tee, Larry was surprised to see Louie standing there with not one but two caddies by his side. They teed off and got about half way around the course when Larry's curiosity couldn't be contained any longer.

"What's the deal?" asked Larry. "You win the lottery or something?"

"What do you mean?" asked Louie.

"You know what I mean," said Larry. "The two caddies. Why are you using two caddies?"

"Oh, them," said Louie. "My wife was complaining I wasn't spending enough time with the kids."

Two guys were talking in the grillroom at their club over lunch. During the course of their conversation, they touched upon one of the club's better players, Chuck.

"Chuck's playing in the local championship this week," one of the men said matter of factly, and the conversation moved on.

Next week, the same two guys were again having lunch in the grillroom after golf when the conversation again turned to Chuck.

"Chuck's playing in the state championship this week," the first guy again mentioned matter of factly, and like the week before, the conversation moved on.

A week later they're having lunch again in the grillroom after golf, and the conversation once again turns to Chuck.

"Say," said the first guy, "Chuck's playing in the regional championship this week."

"Help me out here," the second guy said. "There's something I don't understand. Every week when we're having lunch, you tell me what Chuck is doing. How come you know his schedule so well?"

"I have to know it," said the first guy, "I'm seeing his wife!"

148

A twosome was finishing up on the fifteenth hole as the weather began to turn. A big storm was blowing their way. As they walked off the green towards the next tee, one of the fellows turned to his friend and asked him what he scored on the hole.

"I got a four," he said.

Suddenly the sky darkened, and from the heavens a bolt of lightning came crashing down from the sky nearly striking him.

"Okay, okay," shook the man, "make it a five."

149

Paul was having a rough time trying to figure out how to teach himself how to play golf. After months of frustration, his wife suggested that, once and for all, he should either take some lessons or just give it up, because he obviously wasn't getting anywhere this way. At first Paul didn't want to hear it (kind of like getting a man to stop to ask for directions when he's lost), but, eventually, it became obvious even to him that he wasn't getting anywhere, so he finally agreed to take some lessons. He went to see the local pro and signed up to begin the following week.

The day of the first lesson arrived, and Paul met the pro at the clubhouse and they proceeded out to the practice tee. When they arrived at the practice tee, Paul put down his bag and took a bucket of balls to his station, throwing a few on the ground.

"Not so fast," said the pro. "First things first. Let's start by swinging the club without hitting anything."

"For God's sake," cried Paul, "that's why I'm here to begin with!"

150

The dumb golfer came running into the clubhouse one afternoon.

"I shot a hole-in-one, I shot a hole-on-one," he shouted for all in the room to hear.

Everyone in the room congratulated him as they headed into the bar for free drinks.

They were drinking in the bar and talking to the dummy about his shot when a perplexed look suddenly came across his face.

"What's the matter?" one of the people asked him.

"It's my hole-in-one," he said. "It's probably the only one I'll ever get. I can't for the life of me figure out how in the world I'm going to mount it."

151

Jeff and Mark finished their weekly round of golf with Jeff pulling out his typical victory, although not by the customary wide margin. Even though the match was unusually close, Mark seemed more upset than usual by the outcome.

"Talk about the worst luck in the world," grumbled Mark as they headed into the locker room. "I just can't seem to buy a damn break."

"Why are you being so hard on yourself?" asked Jeff. "You played great this week. Heck, you almost actually won."

"That's what's so aggravating," cried Mark, "I cheated like crazy, and I *still* lost!"

152

The foursome teed off on the long par three eighth hole. As it happened, the green on this particular par three lay behind a large bunker, so any shot that made the green would disappear over the bunker. You couldn't tell where your ball landed until you arrived on the green. After the last player hit his shot, the guy that hit first charged off down the fairway, without waiting for the others.

He vanished over the bunker and moments later came running back down the fairway towards the other three, jumping and screaming, "I got a hole-in-one! I don't believe it! I got a hole-in-one!"

"You've got to be kidding," said the other three players, as they reached the green. "You run ahead of us down the fairway. Then you disappear over the rise, where you know we can't see you, and, all of a sudden, you start hootin' and hollerin' about a hole-in-one. Do you actually expect us to believe you? How stupid do you think we are?"

"No, no. It's true. I swear it," he said crossing his heart. "Go look. I left it in the hole to prove it."

153

The golfer's investments weren't doing particularly well, so one afternoon he called up his broker to complain.

"How's it going?" he asked when his broker came on the line.

"Great!" said the broker. "I broke eighty today."

"That's the reason I'm calling," said the man. "It seems I'm one of them."

154

A young man was paired with three really old men for a round of golf. Before they teed off on the first hole, the old fellows asked the youngster if he would be interested in making the round a little more interesting.

"Sure," he chuckled. "What are the stakes?"

"We play pinochle golf," said one of the men.

"Pinochle golf?" said the young man. "I don't think I've ever heard of pinochle golf. How does it work?"

"It's a simple game," said another of the old guys. "We play a dollar a hundred!"

155

Two girlfriends were talking over coffee one morning.

"Your husband plays a lot of golf, doesn't he?" the first woman asked.

"He sure does, and his betting has become a problem," said the second woman.

"You mean he plays for money?" asked the first woman.

"That's the problem," said the second woman. "The chump plays *for* money all the time. Unfortunately, he never *wins* any!"

The poor hacker couldn't hit the proverbial broad side of a barn. What made it even worse was that on this particular occasion, his caddie couldn't control his laughter. After just about every shot, he had to contend with the chuckles and snorts. Finally, after three hours of enduring this abuse, he lost it.

He turned to the caddie and said, "That's it. I've had just about all that I'm going to take from you. I'm warning you. If you laugh one more time I'm going to knock your block off!"

The caddie just grinned.

"I doubt you'd know which club to use, sir," he said. "And even if you did, I'd wager you'd probably miss!"

157

The dentist received a phone call as he was right in the middle of working on a patient.

"Uh huh," he said, "I see. Don't worry. I'll be right there."

He hung up the phone, took off his mask and gloves, went into the closet, grabbed his golf clubs, and proceeded to head out of the office.

"My God, Doctor," exclaimed his shocked nurse, "where are you going?"

"It's an emergency," said the doctor, racing through the door. "I have eighteen cavities to fill!"

158

It was rapidly approaching that time of year again. The nine millionth annual golf championship of heaven. This year, as usual, the two teams were to be fielded by St. Peter and Jesus. The rules of the tournament were simple. Anyone was eligible to play, as long as he was a man of the cloth. Now this presented a problem every year for St. Peter because Jesus always seemed to get to all the best players first, and St. Peter's man invariably would lose the championship. Well, this year St. Peter was determined that his player was going to win. Even if he was forced to stretch the rules.

The opening day of the tournament came, and St. Peter was already waiting out on the first tee when Jesus arrived.

"Good morning, Lord," St. Peter said to Jesus as He arrived at the first tee. "Nice day for a golf match. Isn't it?"

"Why it certainly is," replied Jesus. "Is your man ready?"

"He sure is," said St. Peter, barely able to contain the smirk that was spreading across his face. "I'd like you to meet my player, Cardinal Daly."

"It's a pleasure to meet you, my son," said Jesus. "May I wish you all the best."

Then Jesus turned to St. Peter, who by now could no longer hold back the grin on his face.

"Peter," said Jesus, "Now I'd like you to meet *my* player. Come on out here, *Archbishop Couples!*"

159

The golf nut was out on a first date with a beautiful woman, and naturally the subject of conversation turned to golf. This guy was going on and on about the courses he'd played, the type of equipment he used, talking about all kinds of different shots, and, in general, just going on and on. Much to his delight, as he continued to talk, this gorgeous lady was staring at him intently and smiling and nodding her head in agreement with everything he said. He was absolutely thrilled that not only was he out with this stunning creature, but that she actually seemed to share his love of golf. It all seemed too good to be true.

"But enough talk about me," he said. "Tell me. How long have you been playing golf?"

"Golf?" she asked. "What's golf?"

160

After another poor showing on the course, the golfer was complaining to his friend.

"That's it," he said. "This is all getting me nowhere. I think it's time that I took a golf psychiatry course."

"Why," asked his friend, "so you can improve your mind?"

"No," he said. "So I can find out why I'm letting this stupid game drive me *out of it*!"

161

"I can't stand golf jokes," one golfer said to another.

"Why not?" said the other golfer.

"Because," he said, "they're always beating me!"

Ernie was paired together with another fellow for a round of golf. As it happened, they were both eighteen handicaps, so they decided to make the round a little more interesting and play for some money. Round about the eighth hole, however, Ernie began to suspect something was rotten on the course. This guy was making shots from all over the course. Either his opponent was having the round of his life, or else he was Joe Sandbag and old Ernie was getting hustled. The thought did not sit well with Ernie, but he decided not to say anything, just in case the guy really was just having a lucky day.

He kept the thought until the sixteenth hole. The sixteenth was a long par five dogleg left, with trees on either side. They teed off, and both their tee shots failed to clear the dogleg. When they arrived at their balls, this guy pulled out a one iron (that was the other clue something was amiss) and proceeded to blast a low draw around the trees. The ball rolled onto the green and came to rest six inches from the hole. Ernie just stood there and stared daggers at this guy. The guy looked back at Ernie and laughed nervously.

"Gee," he said, "someone up there must like me."

"Yeah," said Ernie, heading towards him, "and you're just about on the way to meet Him!"

Frank arrived home from the golf course after his usual Sunday game.

"So how was your golfing today?" his wife asked, as he came through the door.

"Most interesting," said Frank. "I played golf today with the most amazing guy in the world."

"What was so amazing about him?" asked his wife. "Was it his driving?"

"No," said Frank.

"Was it his iron play?" she asked.

"Nope," said Frank.

"So he must have been a great putter?" she asked.

"Uh, uh," he said.

"So then, what was so amazing about him?" she asked.

"You wouldn't have believed it," said Frank. "He actually kept score in pen!!"

164

Two chauvinistic guys were sitting and talking in the grillroom after golf.

"I think I've figured out why women play golf," said the first guy.

"And why would that be?" queried the second.

"It gives them something to lie about other than their age."

165

Albert was talking to his friend about his marital woes.

"I can't believe it," he said. "After all these years, my wife told me she'd had it with my golfing. She said she wasn't going to put up with it anymore, and that I was going to have to make a choice. It was either going to be her, or the golf."

"So what did you tell her?" his friend asked.

"What do you think I told her?" said Albert. "I told her I was really going to miss her."

166

It was the talk of the club. Tom had been a member for years, and everyone knew and liked him, so it came as quite a shock when the members learned that he had committed suicide.

"What in the world do you think would make him do something like that?" one of the members asked.

"I heard a rumor," said another of the members.

"What was it?" he was asked.

"I heard that he passed on an opportunity to buy Callaway stock at two!"

167

The young golfer had just won his first regional tournament and was cornered in the parking lot of the course by a golf groupie—a very attractive woman.

"Say, big fella," she purred into his ear, "are you as much a champion off the course as you are on it?"

Not being one to decline a challenge, he leaned over and said to her, "There's only one way to find out."

And with that, they hopped into her car, and headed off to her apartment. When they arrived at her place, they went upstairs and made mad, crazy love. After they finished, and he was resting on the pillows, she leaned over to him.

"You call yourself a champion?" she cooed. "Arnold Palmer wouldn't have quit this fast."

Not wanting to be called a quitter, he rolled over and they

went at it again. Afterwards, as he lay resting, she again sidled over to him.

"You call yourself a champion?" she whispered. "Jack Nicklaus wouldn't have quit this fast."

With his reputation on the line, he took a deep breath, and once again dove into the fray. Afterwards, as he lay there gasping for air, she again curled up next to him.

"You call yourself a champion?" she purred. "Nick Faldo wouldn't have quit this fast."

"For God's sake, lady," he croaked, "what the hell is par around here?!"

168

Bob was sitting around the house one Saturday, doing nothing but being cranky.

"What's the matter with you?" his wife asked.

"There's nobody for me to play golf with," he grumbled.

"Why don't you call up George?" she suggested. "I spoke to his wife this morning, and she told me he was home and had no plans."

"Forget it," Bob snapped. "Would you play golf with a guy who cheats?"

"Oh, my," said his wife. "I wasn't aware of that. No, I guess I wouldn't."

"Well," he said, "neither would George."

169

The storm clouds were gathering, and the foursome was trying to finish their round before the rains came. Unfortunately, in the group in front of them one of the players was so slow he was mucking up things for everyone. They finally couldn't stand it anymore, and one of them screamed down the fairway for him to please pick it up a bit. The slowpoke just turned around, made a gesture, and yelled back something about playing as slow as he wanted, and who was going to do anything about it if they didn't like it?

Suddenly, a huge bolt of lightning came crashing down from the sky, lifting the slowpoke into the air, and sending him thirty yards down the fairway.

"Wow," said one of the guys to the others. "Heck of a penalty for slow play."

170

First golfer: "So, how's your handicap these days?"
Second golfer: "It's scratch."
First golfer: "Really?"
Second golfer: "Yeah, I keep the scores I like, and scratch out the bad ones."

171

Golfer's prayer when his wife takes up the game:
"Dear Lord, please don't let her be better than I!"

172

After a great evening out, the golfer and his date spent the night together for the first time. In the morning, over coffee, she remarked to him:

"Gee, you were really great last night," she said. "I'd never been with a golfer before. You were wonderful. What's your secret?"

"Oh, it's no secret," he said. "It's just good course management."

173

"How come you play so much golf?" his wife complained.

"'Cause it's good for me," her husband replied.

"And what makes it so good for you?" she asked.

"Because," he said, "I get to spend time in the fresh air and lie in the sun!"

174

A fellow played a resort course in Florida where the sixteenth hole was a par three with an island green.

"You know, sir," his caddie said, as they arrived on the tee, "Tom Watson played this course just last week."

"That's nice," the fellow said as he teed up his ball. He took his swing and watched as the ball sailed high into the air and dropped twenty yards short of the green, into the water. He mumbled something to himself and teed up another ball, took his cut, and again watched as the ball flew into the air, only to plop again into the water. This time he cursed out loud, as he teed up yet another ball. He took his swing and watched forlornly as, once again, the ball rose high into the air only to come down smack into the water. With that, he turned to his caddie.

"That's it," he said. "I give up. What did Watson use when he played this hole?"

"An old ball."

175

A husband and wife were playing in a mixed pairs tournament at their local club. The first hole was a par four. The husband played first, hitting a beautiful tee shot smack down the middle of the fairway. They got to the ball, and his wife took out her three wood and proceeded to hit the ball twenty yards into a nearby fairway bunker. Her husband took out his five iron, stepped in, and hit a lovely shot out of the bunker just short of the green. His wife then took her putter and blasted the ball through the green, and into a bunker behind the green. Her husband, biting his lip, said nothing. He took out his sand wedge and played a glorious shot out of the bunker, running the ball across the green and right into the cup.

"I can't believe we started with a bogey," he said to her as they walked off the green.

"Hey," she said, "don't get snippy with me. Only *two* of those shots were mine!"

176

Jim had just finished playing a round of golf and was in the locker room getting undressed to take a shower when one of his friends happened to notice him slipping out of a pair of women's panties.

"Hey, Jimbo," his friend called out across the locker room. "How long have you been playing golf in women's underwear?"

"How long?" came the reply. "Ever since my wife found a pair in the back seat of my car after I came home from supposedly playing a round of golf!"

177

Greg was playing a round of golf with his buddies one morning when they came to the par five fourteenth hole. The fourteenth was a long dogleg right surrounded on both sides by a thick grove of trees. Greg topped his tee shot and sent it running down the fairway, where it stopped about thirty yards short of clearing the dogleg. They got to Greg's ball, and one of his friends told him he might as well just pitch the ball out onto the fairway, since there was no way he was going to be able to get through those trees and onto the green. Greg, however, didn't want to hear it. He didn't want to lose a shot and was positive he could make it through the trees, so he went into his bag and pulled out his trusty three wood. He set up over the ball, drew the club back, and let fly with all his might. The ball took off with a crack, flew to the edge of the trees, hit square off the very first tree and ricocheted right back at Greg, striking him smack in the middle of the forehead, killing him instantly.

The next thing Greg knew, he was standing in front of the Pearly Gates talking with none other than St. Peter.

"Welcome to Heaven, my son," said St. Peter. "Tell me. How did you get here?"

Still a little stunned, Greg looked at St. Peter.

"In two."

178

A group of immigrant laborers got jobs working on a golf course. Having never heard of golf or having never seen a course before, they were amazed at the strangeness of the activity going on around them. Their first day out, they were working around one of the greens when a hacker came down the fairway, hitting his ball (often) as he went. The guy finally got up on the green, and, after some doing, managed to roll his ball into the hole. Watching this whole scenario unfold, one of the workers turned to his friend with a smirk on his face.

"Boy," he said, "now he's in *big* trouble!"

179

"You're going out to play golf again?" his wife complained.

"Don't be angry with me," her husband replied. "I'm only doing it under strict doctor's orders."

"Do I look that stupid?" she said. "You expect me to believe that your doctor told you to play golf?"

"But it's true," he said, as he walked out the front door. "He told me specifically that I should get some iron every day!"

180

"I don't understand you," said his wife. "You spend all this time and money on your precious golf. Sooner or later, you won't be able to play anymore. What will you have saved for that rainy day when it comes?"

"A whole lot of work!"

"Did you hear about the rich golfer?"

"No. How rich was he?"

"He was so rich he hired a full-time caddie to tend his automatic putting machine."

Hal finally got bit by the bug and took up golf. He went out and bought all the equipment and joined a private club. His first time out, he stood on the first tee and tried to tee up his ball. He let go, and it fell off the tee. He bent over again and set it up. Again, it fell off. After three more attempts with no more luck than the first two tries, he turned to his caddie.

"Wow," he said. "People are right. This really *is* a tough game."

183

"There seems to be a problem, my dear," the groom said to his bride. "It looks as it we're going to have to postpone our wedding."

"Postpone our wedding?" came the shocked reply. "Everything's been set for months—the hall, the caterer, the flowers, the music. The whole thing's already been paid for, for God's sake. The invitations went out weeks ago. Why on earth do we have to postpone it?"

"I'm sorry, my darling," he said, "but I just checked a calendar. Our twenty-fifth anniversary falls on a Sunday. I always play golf on Sunday.

184

Jay ran into one of his friends after playing golf on a Sunday.

"So tell me, Jay," his friend said. "I hear you got a new set of sticks."

"That's true," said Jay, "I did."

"And have they helped your game at all?" he asked.

"Oh yeah," said Jay. "They've been a big help. You should see it. They've added at least thirty yards to my slices, almost thirty-five yards to my hooks, and you'd be amazed by the size of my divots."

185

It was a sad sight indeed. After twenty-five years, poor Sean had no choice but to give up his beloved golf game.

Seems he lost his ball!

186

The phone rang in the doctor's office. His nurse answered it. She listened for a few moments, then told the person on the other end of the line to hold on, and she put down the receiver.

"Doctor," she said, "I have a forty-year-old man on the line."

"What's his problem?" asked the doctor.

"He seems to be very sick," she said. "He's complaining his nerves are shot, he can't concentrate, he's shaking all the time, and he keeps vomiting. What should I tell him?"

"That's easy," said the doctor. "Just tell him to take up golf."

"Okay," said the nurse, "but what if he already plays golf?"

"Simple," said the Doc. "Tell him to quit."

187

Glen came home from playing in the local golf tournament.

"How did it go today?" his wife asked him, as he came through the door.

"Not very well," he said. "They had to take Arthur to the hospital in an ambulance."

"My goodness," said his wife. "What happened?"

"He was just having a lousy day," said Glen. "He kept missing shot after shot and the more he'd miss, the more aggravated he'd get, until he finally got so upset with himself that he ruptured a blood vessel and passed right out."

"Why that's terrible," said his wife.

"It sure is," said Glen. "It kind of gives new meaning to the term 'Stroke Play.'"

Two guys were having drinks in a local bar on Long Island late one Saturday night when one of them looked up to see a famous golf pro sitting at a table with three beautiful women. They were laughing and drinking up a storm.

"Hey," the guy said to his friend. "Look over there. Is that who I think it is?"

"Why, I do believe it is," said his friend.

"Isn't he defending his title in the golf tournament tomorrow?"

"Why, I do believe he is," said his friend.

"That's unbelievable," said the first guy. "He's defending in one of the major golf championships in the world tomorrow, and here he is out late the night before the final round drinking and carousing around with three beautiful women. I don't know what to think."

"Hey," said his friend, "I do. I think he has his priorities straight!"

Q: Do golfers live for abuse?

A: Of course they do. Why else would they play a game that spelled backwards is *flog?*

Two friends were having a discussion on the finer reasons why they liked the game of golf.

"What I like about golf," the first guy said, "is that you get to spend the day outdoors in the sun and fresh air, exercising your body and your mind."

"Forget that," said his friend. "I'll tell you why golf is such a great game. Where else can a guy like me get to spend the day with a bunch of hookers and not have his wife kill him!"

A couple of multimillionaires were sitting around the clubhouse at their private golf club, bored to tears.

"You want to go out and play a round of golf?" the first millionaire asked his friend.

"I guess so," said the second millionaire. "What do you want to play for?"

"I don't know," said the first. "How about ten million dollars?"

"Okay," said the second, "but let's bet something else to make it *really* interesting."

"Hmmm," said the first, thinking for a moment. "I've got it! Let's play for a sleeve of *new balls!*"

192

Gladys was talking on the phone with her friend Marge when the subject turned to their husbands' golf games.

"So tell me," said Gladys. "How did your Morris play today?"

"I'll tell you," said Marge. "I don't think he played very well at all today."

"And what makes you say that?" said Gladys.

"I figured it out," said Marge, "when I dumped two pounds of sand out of each of his golf shoes."

193

Q: What's the best tip in golf?

A: The one you give to the starter!

194

The golfer was already buried up to his neck in the quicksand when his partner discovered him.

"My God," his partner yelled. "Whatever you do, don't move. I'll save you. I'll go get a rope and pull you out with the golf cart."

"Forget that," the guy screamed. "Just get me my sand wedge. Fast!"

195

The novice woman golfer came storming into the club-house after making a futile attempt to play a round.

"What an incredible waste," she railed. "All that time and money, shot to Hell. I can't believe it. Those *screwing* lessons were completely worthless. I still can't play golf worth a tinker's damn!"

"Pardon me, ma'am," said one of the other members, interrupting her tirade. "But I couldn't help overhearing your complaining. If you don't mind my saying so, perhaps it would have been more helpful if you had taken *golfing* lessons instead."

196

Two lady friends met at a local restaurant for lunch.

"I hear your husband hasn't been feeling well lately," the first woman said.

"Oh, he was in bad shape there, for a while," her friend replied.

"But he's feeling better now?" she asked.

"Much, much better now, thank you. He's finally, for the first time in his life, completely at peace with himself and the universe around him."

"You don't say," said her friend. "And to what do you credit this remarkable turnaround?"

"It turned out to be quite simple, actually," she said. "He gave up golf!"

197

Two novice women golfers are out on the course one day. The first woman tees up her ball, swings, and watches as it takes off on a ninety-degree angle. It flies about twenty yards, hits a rock, bounces off a nearby cart path, hits a tree, careens off the tree, and finally comes to rest in the middle of the fairway.

"Hey!" says her friend, giving her a miffed look. "Why didn't you tell me you've been practicing?"

198

Two old codgers were sitting around the bar in the grill room one afternoon reminiscing about the good old days.

"Say," said one of them, "I remember the first time I saw one of them miniskirts. It was way back in nineteen-sixty something."

"Yep," said his sidekick, "I don't remember the exact year either. But what I do remember is the first time I saw a girl in one of them. I was on the eighteenth green. It was the only time in my life I missed a six inch putt!"

199

"Do you know what my butcher and my golf game have in common?" a fellow asked his friend.

"No, I don't believe I do," was the reply.

"They both have a slice that costs me a fortune!"

200

"I play golf in the low eighties," the little old man was telling one of the youngsters at his club.

"Wow," said the young man, "that's pretty impressive."

"Not really," said the old guy. "Any hotter and I'd probably have a stroke."

201

The man went to see his doctor. He wasn't feeling at all well. He was tired, run down, and generally suffering from exhaustion.

"My diagnosis is you're worn out," said the doctor. "I believe you've been playing too much golf."

"Too much golf," moaned the patient. "What can I do?"

"You need to take some time off and relax." said the doc. "My advice to you is to go spend some time at the office."

202

A husband and his wife were sitting at the dinner table one evening when she suddenly broke down in tears. Taken completely by surprise, the husband could barely spit out a "What's wrong?"

"I'll tell you what's wrong," she sobbed. "There's no romance left in our marriage. After all these years, I'm just old news to you. You couldn't care less about me. The only thing you care about is your stupid golf. You haven't cared since the day we got married."

"Oh, honey," he said, taking her in his arms. "How could you say such a ridiculous thing. The day we were married is etched in my mind like no other day of my life."

"Do you really mean it?" she sniffled.

"Of course I do," he declared. "How could I ever forget it? We were married the day after I got my first eagle!"

203

The hacker couldn't hit a shot to save his life. After fifteen holes of embarrassment and frustration, he finally turned to his caddie, looking for a little reassurance.

"Could there possibly be anyone playing worse than I?" he asked.

"Anything's possible, sir," replied the caddie, "but I doubt he's out playing today."

204

Bernard was all set to tee off on the first hole on a lovely, spring Sunday morning. Just as he sets up to hit the ball, a beautiful young woman in a wedding gown comes running up onto the tee.

"Bernard, Bernard," she screams. "Today is our wedding day. All the guests are at the church—everyone, my whole family. How can you do this to me?"

"Don't get angry at me. I was very specific," says Bernard. "Only if it rains, I said. Only if it rains!"

Not only was the hacker a lousy golfer, but he was also a nasty son of a gun to boot. He slashed his way around the course all day. His poor caddie was doing a yeoman's job just to keep from smacking this clown. Anyway, they're out on the sixteenth hole and, after several shots, the hacker screws up and actually finds himself on a fairway—or so he thinks.

"Give me my three wood," he said to his caddie.

"Uh, sir," said the caddie, "if you don't mind."

"Don't bother me now," snapped the guy. "Just give me the club."

"But, sir!" he tried again.

"What part of 'don't bother me now' didn't you understand?" growled our hero. "For the first time today, I finally have a shot at a green, and I don't want you messing up my concentration."

"As you wish, sir," sighed the caddie, handing him the wood and moving off to the side.

The hacker took the club in hand, set up the ball, and launched what must have been the most beautiful shot he'd ever hit. The ball sailed high into the air, floating on what only could be described as gossamer wings. It landed softly on the green and rolled straight into the cup.

"I don't believe it. I don't believe it," the hacker screamed with joy, as he started dancing right there in the middle of the fairway. After finally calming down, he turned to his caddie.

"See," he said smugly, "it's a good thing I know what I'm doing. If I had stopped to let you bother me, I never would have made that incredible shot. By the way, what exactly was it that you wanted?"

"What I wanted, sir," said the caddie, "was to let you know that wasn't your ball!"

206

Two friends got together for drinks after a round of golf.

"You know," said the first guy, "I'm not exactly sure, but I think that I may have a case of the yips."

"No kidding," said his friend, "and what makes you think that?"

"Well," he began, "you know the par four fifteenth hole, right?"

"The one with the really flat green?"

"That's the one," he continued. "I hit a beautiful second shot right at the flag. The ball bounced once and rolled up to within one foot of the cup."

"So what happened?"

"I hit my fourth shot from the greenside bunker!"

207

First golfer: "Did you know that there are two things you can do on the course when circumstances permit you to improve your lie?"

Second golfer: "No, I wasn't aware there were *two* things you could do. What are they?"

First golfer: "The first thing you can do is reposition your ball."

Second golfer: "I knew that one. What's the other?"

First golfer: "Just change your score."

208

Two men had been playing golf together for over thirty years. During this time, they never got along and would argue constantly. One day out on the course, they got into another of their stupid arguments over something totally trivial. The rhetoric became more and more heated until it looked as if they were going to actually come to blows.

"Come on, you dirtbag!" one shouted at the other. "You don't scare me one little bit. I'll take your best shot. C'mon, hit me! I dare you!"

Not needing anymore provocation, the other guy started toward his friend. However, just as he got within a few feet, he stopped in his tracks and backed away.

"Hah!" gloated his friend. "I knew you didn't have the guts to do anything!"

"No guts, huh?" he replied. "I'm not as stupid as you think I am. I'm not going to fall into your trap. You *want* me to hit you. And I know why. Because you hope I'll break my hand and have to relearn how to play with a new grip!"

209

The president of the club was taking a new member on a tour of the grounds.

"There goes Father Flynn," the president said. "He's our finest player."

"Really," said the new member. "Isn't it a bit unusual for a priest to be that good as a player?"

"No, not at all," said the president. "If you think about it, it makes perfect sense. Who else would have that much practice keeping his head down."

210

A couple of elders were sitting around bemoaning the onset of the golden years.

"I don't know," said the first fellow, "it seems as each year goes by, my golf game gets worse and worse."

"Aw, come on," said his friend, "how bad could it be?"

"I'll tell you how bad," he replied. "It's gotten so bad, I'm already taking shots against next year's rounds!"

211

The first-time player was out on the course with his caddie for what seemed to be an eternity. As the day was coming to a close, the newbee walked over to his caddie.

"When do you think I'll be able to use my putter?" he asked.

"If all goes well, sir," replied the caddie, "sometime before sunset."

212

Then there was the story about the ex-major-league base-ball player who had a hard time grasping the realities of golf.

"I don't know if I'm gonna be able to do this," he confided to his partner the first time out on the course. "When I played baseball, I had the whole field to hit to. This golf business is totally different. How can I be expected to play a game where every hit *has* to be directly into center field!"

213

"My husband is honest to a fault," the woman was telling her friend. "He always calls a spade a spade."

"How does that affect his golf game?" her friend asked.

"Oh, my," she gasped as her face blushed, "I could never tell you what he calls his golf clubs."

214

Gene was heading off to the golf course on a Saturday morning. He really looked the part. He had the wingtip golf shoes, the bright-colored slacks, the shirt with the alligator on the chest, the wide-brimmed straw hat, and those new, fancy wraparound sunglasses. Yes sir, he really looked the part. His wife was sitting in the kitchen with her friend as he went by.

"My," commented the friend, "your husband must be quite the golfer."

"Yeah," came the reply. "Right up until the time he takes his first swing!"

215

Jack was paired with a recent immigrant from Russia named Constantine for a round of golf at a local public course. As they worked their way around the course, they got to talking.

"Say," commented Jack, "you're a pretty good player. I didn't know they had many good golfers in Russia."

"Of course they do," said Constantine. "I'll bet you didn't know that back home in my country I was a participant in the Russian Open?"

"That's very interesting," said Jack. "I didn't know there was a Russian Open."

"Oh, indeed," replied Constantine. "They opened Russia... and I got out!"

216

Dale and Hale were on the eighteenth green with their match all tied up. Dale's ball lay about twelve feet from the hole. Hale's ball was just inside Dale's ball, on exactly the same line.

Dale lined up his putt, pulled the trigger, and watched mournfully as the ball rolled towards the hole only to break left of the cup and roll on by. Now it was Hale's turn. He set up over the ball, drew the club back slowly, and let it roll. The ball started right for the hole, exactly as Dale's did, and then broke left just before the hole and rolled by, just like Dale's.

"I see you didn't learn much from my putt," said Dale.

"The Hell I didn't," snapped Hale, as he tapped in his ball. "I learned how to miss it!"

217

The self-appointed Blue Bloods were holding court in the grillroom of the club one afternoon discussing the things that they considered to be of the utmost importance.

"All things considered," one of them sniffed, "you must agree, there's really nothing more important than breeding."

"Here, here," his compatriots concurred.

"I don't know, guys," said one of the *common* members who happened to catch all this as he was passing by, "I like breeding as much as the next person, but I also like to get in a little golf every now and again!"

218

It was a Sunday morning and the priest was standing by the eighteenth green, waiting as the young boy came in from finishing a round of golf.

"Young man," said the priest sternly, "it's a Sunday morning and you're out here playing golf when you should be in church giving thanks to the Lord. What would your father have to say about this?"

"I don't know, Father," said the boy. "He's coming in right behind me. Let's ask him."

219

"You know, golf is a little like playing with yourself," said the first fellow.

"Why is that?" asked his friend.

"Because," he said, "while it may be fun for you, it's disgusting for anyone who happens to be watching."

220

Two golfers were talking.

"You know," said the first golfer, "someone should invent a golf ball that squeals when you lose it."

"Why should someone do that?" asked the second golfer.

"Because then the golfer wouldn't have to do it!"

221

A flying saucer from another planet lost control while attempting to land on earth. It crashed into a bunker on a golf course and became stuck. The alien crew radioed their mother ship for assistance.

"Attention, attention. We seem to have gotten ourselves stuck in this very odd hole in the ground," they reported. "How are we to extricate ourselves? Please advise."

Came the response, "Try a wedge!"

222

His wife had enough.

"Golf, golf, golf," she whined. "That's all that's on your silly

little pea brain. You couldn't stop thinking about golf if your life depended on it."

"You think you know it all," came the reply. "I could quit thinking about golf any time I wanted to."

"I bet you couldn't," she said.

"Oh, yeah," he said, "I bet I can...and don't putt it past me!"

223

A man is playing a round of golf solo one day, and probably for good reason. He really stinks. He tees up his ball on the twelfth hole and takes a vicious cut, missing the ball by a foot. He takes swing number two, again missing the ball by a nice margin. He tries swing number three, and whiffs again. Just then, he notices a hunter standing off in the woods watching him.

"Hey," he yells at the hunter, "can't you read the sign. It says 'Golfers Only.'"

"No problem, Buddy," says the hunter. "I won't say anything if you don't."

224

Donnie was playing golf one day with a guy who wouldn't stop talking. All through the round, he just continued to ramble on and on, never once shutting his mouth. Needless to say, this became quite annoying, but Donnie didn't know what to do to shut this guy up. Round about the fifteenth hole, this motor-mouth put his tee shot into a fairway bunker. He was railing on about it the whole way down the fairway. They got to the bunker, and this guy just kept on complaining as he climbed on in.

"I'll tell you," he said, "this trap is really annoying."

"You're right about that," said Donnie, seizing the opportunity, "and I'd appreciate it if you'd kindly *keep yours shut!*"

225

Before Bobby turned in his scorecard, his partner took a look at it.

"You got a *fifteen* on the eighteenth hole!" he said in shock. "How in the name of Heaven did you get a fifteen?"

"How do you think I got a fifteen, smart guy?" came the snotty reply. "I missed my putt for fourteen!"

226

Two men were leaving church on a bright Sunday morning.

"You know," said the first fellow, "I can always tell who the golfers are in church."

"You can?" said his pal. "How can you tell that?"

"It's easy," he said. "You just look to see who prays with an interlocking grip."

227

Two lady friends were talking after witnessing the final round of the local club golf tournament.

"There's something interesting I've noticed about men when they play golf," the first lady said to her friend.

"And what might that be?" her friend asked.

"I've noticed that whenever they miss a shot, they manage to find some excuse, and end up blaming it all on fate."

"Yeah, so?"

"But should they manage to get lucky and hit a good shot, suddenly, they're chalking it up to their boundless skill."

228

Two old friends meet on the street one day in their village.

"So how goes the old golf game?" the first guy asks.

"Great!" says the second guy. "I've been shooting in the low seventies."

"Honestly?" says the first.

"What's that got to do with it?"

229

Sheldon called Wayne on the phone the other morning.

"I had the most incredible dream last night," Sheldon said. "I dreamt that I was playing golf on the most beautiful golf course on the entire planet, and I had the place all to myself."

"That's nice," said Wayne. "You're on the most spectacular golf course in the world, and you don't bother to call your best friend to invite him to join you. Nice guy."

"I'm sorry," said Sheldon, "I just didn't think of it. Please forgive me."

"Aw, that's okay," said Wayne. "I couldn't have played anyway. As it happens, last night I had a dream where I spent the night with two of the sexiest, most beautiful women on the face of the earth."

"Hey!" snipped Sheldon. "You complain about me not calling you, and you go and spend the night with two of the hottest women on the planet and you don't bother to call me?"

"Don't get testy with me," said Wayne. "I *did* call you last night."

"You did?" said Sheldon. "What happened?"

"I spoke to your wife," said Wayne. "She said you were playing golf!"

230

Neil's wife was waiting for him at the front door when he arrived home from the course, and she was not pleased.

"If you aren't the biggest good-for-nothing so-and-so I've ever known," she started in as he walked through the door. "You know damn well that you were supposed to be home from the golf course hours ago. You knew that we had plans to go out, but, once again, you managed to completely screw things up. I'm totally disgusted with you. What do you have to say for yourself?"

"Bennie had a heart attack and died on the second hole."

"Oh my God," said his wife, "that's terrible."

"You're telling me," said Neil. "That's what slowed us

down. The whole rest of the round it was 'Hit the ball, drag Bennie, hit the ball, drag Bennie...'"

231

A man was paired with a priest for a round of golf one morning. They headed out onto the course, and it became fairly evident right away that the priest wasn't much of a golfer. As a matter of fact, he was downright lousy. He'd chunk almost every shot, and, much to this guy's amazement, launch into a veritable tirade of profanities the likes of which this poor fellow had never heard from regular folks, much less than from a man of the cloth. Finally after fourteen holes of this ranting, raving and all-around carrying on, the priest confided in the man.

"You know, my son," he said, "this just isn't going to work. I can't see any alternative, but to give it up."

"Give up golf, Father?" said the man.

"No," he said, "the priesthood!"

232

Wife to Husband: "So Dear, how did your golf game go?"

Husband to Wife: "Not so great. I fanned on so many shots, my poor caddie caught pneumonia."

233

The twosome came to a long par three with a large pond protecting the green.

"Damn," said the first fellow. "I hate these holes with water hazards. I always end up losing a new ball. I can't stand that."

"What's the big deal," said the second fellow. "Just use an old ball."

"I'm not stupid," said the first fellow. "That's just what I'd do, except for one thing."

"What's that?" he asked.

"I've never had an old ball!"

234

Two golfers finished up on the ninth green and headed over to the tenth tee.

"What did you get on that hole?" asked the first golfer.

"I shot a four," said the second.

"Hey, wait a minute," said the first. "I counted you taking five strokes. What gives? You're not trying to cheat, are you?"

"Of course not," said the second guy. "My first swing was only a practice swing."

"If your first swing was only a practice swing," said the first guy, "then why did you feel the need to yell 'Dammit'?"

235

"My doctor told me I needed to exercise and lose weight," a man was telling his friend, "so I took up golf."

"That's great," said his friend. "How's it going?"

"Not so good," he replied. "Since I started playing and finished stocking the little cart you ride around in, I've managed to put on twelve pounds."

236

Two friends are playing the seventeenth hole when one of them slices his ball into the bushes. He goes into the bushes to retrieve his ball. Suddenly, from somewhere in the undergrowth, a snake jumps out and bits him smack on his butt. Needless to say, he lets out quite a shriek, which causes his friend to come running over.

"What happened?" his friend called into the bushes.

"I was looking for my ball when this snake jumped out of nowhere and bit me on the butt!" he cried.

"Don't worry," his friend said, "I just saw Dr. Davis walking off the eighteenth green. Let me run over and try and catch him. He'll know what to do."

"Fine. Just please hurry," the poor guy moaned.

His friend raced to the parking lot, caught Dr. Davis and apprised him of the situation.

"I'll call an ambulance," said Dr. Davis. "But if you want your friend to live, you're going to have to get back to him quickly, cut a small incision in the bite mark, and suck out the poison."

With that, the friend ran back to the guy waiting in the woods.

"Did you catch the doctor?" asked the victim.

"Yes, I did," said the friend.

"Well for goodness' sake," he groaned, "what did he say?"

"He said you're going to die!"

237

Poor old Ted was scheduled to compete in the local golf club championship, something he was not exactly looking forward to. He decided it might not be a bad idea to get out on the course a few days early to sharpen his stroke, so he wouldn't embarrass himself during the competition. Not wanting to leave anything to chance, he figured it would be a smart move to bring a caddie along to check his swing and for a little positive reinforcement. As they were about midway through the back nine, the subject of the upcoming competition came up.

"Tell me," Ted said to his caddie. "You've worked at the club for a number of years. What kind of information can you give me about my opponent?"

"Oh, he really stinks," said the caddie. "He has an unbelievable slice, can't hit out of the rough or a bunker to save his life, and he putts like he's playing in the dark."

"That's great!" said Ted, his spirits soaring.

"Not really, sir," responded the caddie. "He's gonna trash you."

238

The secretary of the private golf club was out walking the grounds one foggy morning, as was his custom, when he came upon a homeless person fast asleep behind a bunker next to the fifteenth green. In a rather loud and abrupt way, he announced himself as the club secretary and informed the man that this behavior of his was entirely unacceptable. Waking with a start, the homeless man jumped to his feet.

"Well let me tell *you* something, Mr. Secretary," said the man rubbing his eyes and stretching. "This is no way to attract new members!"

239

The day after her husband's untimely death, the widow Goldberg met with the funeral director.

"What would you like to say in the obituary?" he asked.

"Goldberg died," she replied.

"That's really a bit short, Mrs. Goldberg," said the funeral director. "Isn't there anything you might want to add?"

"All right," said Mrs. Goldberg. "How about, 'Goldberg died. Golf clubs for sale.'"

240

A man went to see his priest with a question that had been troubling him for quite some time.

"Father," said the man, "I need you to answer an important question for me."

"What is your question, my son?" asked the priest.

"Father," asked the man, "I need to know if there is a golf course in Heaven."

"That is indeed a profound question, my son," replied the priest. "I'll need a little time to get an answer for you on that one. Come back and see me tomorrow after services, and I'll have an answer for you."

The next morning right after services, the priest found the man anxiously waiting for him outside the church.

"Good morning, Father," said the man. "Do you have an answer for me?"

"Yes, my son, I do," said the priest. "I have some good news for you, and also some bad news."

"Well, okay Father," said the man. "What's the good news?"

"The good news, my son," said the priest, "is that there is indeed a most beautiful course in heaven. The most glorious course in all of creation."

"Why, that's wonderful," said the man, breathing a sigh of relief. "So what's the bad news?"

"It seems you'll be teeing off there at 9:00 A.M. tomorrow."

241

And then there was the one about the not entirely bright golddigger who instantly took up golf one day. Seems she overheard two people talking about finding a diamond in the rough!

242

A few of the guys were having drinks in the clubhouse bar after a round of golf, just kind of shooting the breeze, when the subject of one of the other members came up.

"Did you hear about that sneaky Carl?" the first guy asked.

"Is he the guy who moves mountains with every shot?" the next guy asked.

"That's him," said the first. "I always thought he was a lousy player, but evidently there was a method his madness."

"How's that?" asked one of the other guys.

"I saw him on the course the other day," continued the first guy. "He swung his club and took another of his monster divots, and I just happened to notice that after he picked up the divot and walked back to where he'd taken it from, he didn't replace it. He sort of glanced around to see if anyone was looking and then proceeded to stuff the divot into his golf bag. Naturally, this aroused my curiosity, so I followed him home from the course and what do you think I discovered?"

"What?" asked the others.

"That son of a gun had resodded his entire lawn!"

243

Two women were sitting around the breakfast table one morning discussing the golf habits of their respective husbands.

"My husband," said the first woman, "is up to playing thirty-six holes a day, roughly speaking."

"Oh, really," said the second woman. "But tell me, how many holes does he play without cursing?"

244

A couple of Japanese businessmen were getting set to tee off at their country club one morning, when one of their friends came walking over to them, muttering to himself.

"What's the matter?" one of the men asked his friend.

"It's this darned language thing," said the friend. "It happens every time I get into a bunker."

"*What* happens every time you get into a bunker?" his friend asked.

"Every time I get into a bunker," he said, "I call out for my caddie to get me a sand wedge."

"So what's the problem?"

"The problem," he said, "is that he always turns around, and walks off the course leaving me standing there in the bunker. He comes back fifteen minutes later with a ham and Swiss on rye!"

245

A priest had the day off, so he decided it would be nice to go play a round of golf. He was warming up on the first tee when a young man came over and introduced himself, telling the priest that he's been paired with him for the round.

"That will be lovely," said the priest, "but I just want you to know that I'm fairly new to the game, and that I'll try not to hold you up."

"Not to worry, Father," said the young man, "I'm used to it. I happen to be a golf pro. If there's anything you need to know or if you have any questions, please feel free to ask me. I'd be happy to help you in any way I can."

"Why, thank you," said the priest. "That would be very much appreciated."

And off they went.

During the course of the round, the priest asked many questions, and the young pro gave him all sorts of swing tips and advice. They had a nice time together, and, at the eighteenth green, the priest thanked the young man for his help and turned to walk away.

"Just a minute, Father," the young man said.

"Yes, my son," said the priest.

"You owe me fifty dollars," said the fellow.

"I owe you fifty dollars?" said the priest, obviously taken aback. "Why do I owe you fifty dollars?"

"You owe me fifty dollars," said the young man, "because before we began I told you that I was a golf pro. This is what I do for a living, and since I did help you during the round, it's only right that I get paid for my services."

"Very well, my son," said the priest, more than a little bit annoyed, "but I don't have that much money on me right now. If you would be able to stop by the church tomorrow before services, I'll see that you get your money."

"That would be fine," said the young man, as he turned to walk away. "I'll see you tomorrow."

"Oh, by the way," said the priest, "don't forget to bring your mother and father with you tomorrow when you come to the church."

"My mother and father?" asked the young man quizzically. "Why should I bring my mother and father?"

"I'll marry them for you!"

246

Stella and Harry were the cutest, nicest little old couple you'd ever want to meet—and how they loved their golf. They were never really well off, but they always found the money to play their beloved game. Even though they had to make sacrifices and they only got to play on courses that weren't particularly good, it really didn't matter to them, just as long as they got to play. Well, with both of them being well into their eighties, it was just a matter of time before they passed from this world into the next. As fate would have it, they passed on together and found themselves standing at the gates of Heaven. St. Peter was waiting to greet them when they arrived.

"Stella and Harry, we've been waiting for you," he said. "Because of the way you lived your lives on earth, we want you to know that now that you've arrived, you'll be well taken care of for all eternity."

With that he led them through the Pearly Gates and over to what could only be described as the most beautiful golf course imaginable, and alongside the first fairway, stood a magnificent home.

"This is all yours," said St. Peter. "We truly hope that you enjoy it."

"You can't be serious," exclaimed Stella. "I can't believe it. It's too wonderful."

Harry just stood there in silence.

"Oh Harry, let's go out and play right away," Stella said and turned to St. Peter. "Would it be all right?"

"Of course it would," said St. Peter, leading them around to the side of the house where their own private golf cart sat waiting for them with two new sets of clubs strapped to the back, glistening in the sunlight.

So off they went. They both teed off on the fifth hole and had gone over to Harry's ball when Stella noticed that Harry, who up till now still hadn't said a single word, was just standing over his ball.

Stella walked over to him, put her arm around his shoulder and asked, "Is everything all right, dear?"

Harry turned and slowly looked up at Stella. She was shocked to see his face turn bright red with a rage she had never before seen. (You must realize that here's a man who in over sixty years of marriage never so much as raised an eyebrow in anger, and now he was standing in the middle of this fairway looking like he was about to burst an artery.)

"Is everything all right?!" he exploded. "For sixty years, all I

ever heard was 'Don't drink, don't smoke, don't eat all those fatty foods, watch your cholesterol, watch your blood pressure, drive carefully, get enough sleep, don't get stressed, life is sacrifice.' Dammit, Stella, if you had just left me alone, *we could have been here forty years ago!!*"

247

Two friends were talking in the locker room at their club one day, when the name of one of their friends came up.

"That Jon is the luckiest so-and-so I've ever had the misfortune to play a round of golf with," said the first fellow.

"Why do you say that?" asked his friend.

"It's amazing," said the first. "Every time he'd hit his ball into the rough, he'd go in to find it, and without fail he'd always find it sitting *directly* on someone else's lost tee!"

248

Sam had been playing golf for well over forty years, and in all that time, his wife had never once seen him play. One day after she brought this little fact to his attention, he figured it might not be a bad idea to invite her out to the course to see him in action. When they arrived at the course, Sam went off to get ready in the locker room and told his wife to meet him on the first tee. As Sam got ready to tee off, he suggested to his wife that she walk down the fairway a little way to spot his tee shot. She said okay and walked out about one hundred and fifty yards down the left side of the fairway and waved for him to go ahead and hit. Naturally, he wanted to impress her, so he reared back and put everything he had into his shot. Unfortunately, he hit a low hook that flew like it was on a clothesline directly at his poor wife, who never even had a chance to react. The ball smashed into her head, killing her instantly.

The next day, Sam's at the funeral home making the necessary arrangements when the mortician came out from the back where he's preparing the body for burial. He asks Sam if he can ask him a question.

"I'm so sorry for your loss, sir," he began. "I'm aware of the circumstances surrounding your wife's death, but there is something that, for the life of me, I can't figure out. As I was working on your wife's body, I was quite surprised to come across a *second* golf ball lodged in her navel. I was wondering if you had any idea where it could have come from?"

"Oh, that," said Sam. "That was my Mulligan!"

The reverend awoke on Christmas morning and looked out his window to see what was promising to be a gorgeous day. He couldn't resist the temptation and decided to sneak down to the local golf course to play a round. Naturally, since it was Christmas, there was no one else out on the course, so he had the place all to himself. Now you must understand, that up until today, the reverend had never been much of a golfer, but on this particular day, you'd have thought he'd just taken time off from the P.G.A. tour. He was hitting incredible shot after incredible shot. Greens in regulation, birdies, even an eagle—the whole nine yards. In short, he was having the round of a lifetime, which, as fate would have it, was not going unnoticed up in Heaven. God and the angels were watching. As this wonderful round continued to unfold, the angels viewed it all with more than a bit of consternation, and they finally felt the need to voice their concerns.

"Lord," the angels said, "this man is committing a most grievous sin in our eyes, yet you continue to reward him with incredible play. Why, Lord? Why?"

And the Lord just looked over at the angels with the all-knowing smile that is His alone.

"Relax," He said. "Who's he going to tell?"

250

Moses, Jesus, and a little old man got together for a round of golf one day. When they came to the first of the par threes, which happened to be about 160 yards with a carry over a pond, Moses hit first. He hit a low grounder that headed right for the water. When the ball got to the edge, the water miraculously parted, and the ball rolled through the pond and up onto the green.

Next it was Jesus' turn. He got up and hit almost the exact same shot as Moses, except when his ball reached the pond, it simply rolled across the top of the water and up onto the green.

Now it was the little old man's turn and wouldn't you know, he goes ahead and hits the same shot as the other two, except his ball rolls to a stop just in front of the water. All of a sudden, a fish pop it's head out of the pond, picks up the little old man's ball, and swims it across to the other side and spits it out onto the green. There, from seemingly nowhere, a rabbit appears. The rabbit proceeds to pick up the ball in his mouth, hops over to the hole, and drops it into the cup for a hole in one.

As the three of them head down the fairway, Jesus turns to the little old man.

"Nice shot, Dad."

251

Four guys decide to play a round of golf on New Year's Day. They agree to meet in the clubhouse at six in the morning. One of the men is already sitting at a table, nursing a cup of coffee, when the second fellow comes in and sits down.

"So tell me," he says to his buddy, "how did you manage to get away from the missus?"

"Let me tell you," he said, "it wasn't easy. I had to buy her a new full-length Sable coat."

"Ouch!" said the first guy, as the third friend walked in and sat down at the table.

"So what did you have to do to get out?" they asked him.

"I had to buy my wife a matching diamond necklace and earrings," he groaned.

"That must have smarted," said the first guy, as the fourth friend walked in and plopped himself down at the table.

"Tell us," they said, "what did you have to do to get away from your wife today?"

"All I gotta say is, I better play really well because it cost me a new Mercedes to get away today."

"Yeow!" said the first guy, as the other three turned to him.

"So," they asked him, "how did *you* manage to get yourself out here?"

"There was nothing to it," he smirked. "At four o'clock this morning, I rolled over to my wife and tapped her on the shoulder. She lifted her head and said, 'What do you want?' I said to her, 'Intercourse or the golf course.' With that she put her head back down on the pillow and said, 'It's cold outside. Make sure you bundle up.'"

252

Mr. Conrad, one of the wealthiest men in the state, was a golfing fanatic. He lived in a huge home on the eighteenth fairway of the fanciest, most exclusive golf course in the area with his wife, servants and his beloved dog, Divot.

One morning at breakfast, he was perusing one of the major golf publications, when he happened across an advertisement that caught his attention.

The ad read: "Attention golfers, we will teach your dog to be a reliable and trustworthy caddie. So that the animal can be competent in relaying the necessary information, such as distances and club selection, we will, for no extra charge, teach him to speak English. In addition, he will also learn our super secret technique guaranteed to *immediately* take *at least ten strokes* off your game. The cost for the three-week training is $25,000.

Money back if not completely satisfied," and it was signed "Creshaw's Canine Caddies" with a Las Vegas address.

Conrad was fascinated by the advertisement, and, since money was no object, he got in touch with the school that day and made a reservation for Divot in the next available class. He then summoned his faithful driver, Charles, gave him the $25,000 in cash along with an additional $10,000 to cover expenses, put the dog and driver in his limousine, and sent them off to Las Vegas.

Charles and Divot arrived in Vegas sometime the following day. They checked into the hotel, and, while Divot sat in the room, Charles went directly to the casino where, in the course of three weeks' time, he managed to lose the entire $35,000. Having no money left to pay the hotel bill and not wanting to end up in jail, Charles, who by now was quite desperate, was forced to sell Divot to a visiting tourist couple from Iowa. He then loaded up his luggage and headed home.

Upon his return home, he was not surprised to find Mr. Conrad waiting for him as he entered the house.

"So tell me, Charles," said Mr. Conrad, as Charles brought his bags in, "how did it go?"

"Very well, sir," Charles replied.

"Divot learned how to caddie?" Conrad asked.

"That he did, sir," said Charles.

"And he learned to speak English?"

"It seems a little too well, sir," said Charles.

"What does that mean?" asked Mr. Conrad. "And speaking of Divot, where is he?"

"Therein hangs the tale, sir," said Charles, as he began to fidget. "It seems the school did too good a job with him. He really became quite a good caddie, and in the car on the way home he sat up front with me telling me how he couldn't wait to get home to see you and help you with your game. Then all of a sudden, from out of nowhere, he said to me, 'You know what, Charles? I think that instead of talking golf when we get home, I think the first thing I'll do is tell Mr. Conrad about how Mrs. Conrad has been having an affair with his best friend.'"

"Well, sir," continued Charles, "it was painfully clear to me that something had happened at that school that had evidently caused his poor little doggie brain to fail, and I decided then and there to put the poor animal out of his misery. It was late at night when we came to a bridge over a large river. There were no other cars on the road, so I did what I had to do. I pulled over to the side of the road, went around to the passenger side of the car, opened the door, took him by the collar and flung him over the railing into the river below, where he drowned."

"Oh, to lose my poor Divot, and to find out that my wife is unfaithful, that is too much," said Mr. Conrad, as his eyes began to fill. He then walked over to Charles and while wiping a tear from his eye, leaned over and whispered into his ear, "Divot didn't happen to mention anything about a secret technique, did he?"

253

Mr. Davis was in his office one day when he received a phone call from his biggest customer, Mr. Goldberg. Goldberg was an Eastern European immigrant who came to this country some thirty-five years ago and did very well for himself in business.

"Hello, Mr. Goldberg," said Mr. Davis. "What can I do for you today?" he inquired.

"Davis," said Goldberg, "I vant to play some golf dis veekend. I'd like you should be kind enough to set me up an appointment to play at your club this Sunday."

"Mr. Goldberg," said Davis, "nothing would make me happier than to have you play at my club, but as you know, the club is restricted, and while we *are* working to change that policy, as of now, there's really nothing that I can do."

"Davis," said Goldberg, "let me ask on you a qvestion."

"Yes, Mr. Goldberg," said Davis, "what's the question?"

"Vee do qvite a bit of business together, yes?"

"Yes, Mr. Goldberg, we do."

"And I'm being safe in assuming zat you vish to continue doing this business?"

"Yes, Mr. Goldberg, you are."

"Then you should please be kind enough to make for me an appointment to play at your club this Sunday."

"I'll tell you what," said Davis after a moment's thought, "I'll make a tee-off time under one condition."

"Vhat's the condition?" said Goldberg.

"The condition is that no matter what happens, you can't open your mouth. If anyone hears that accent of yours, they'll beat you up on the spot and throw me out of the club."

"It's a deal," said Goldberg. "Not a void vill escape mine lips. Not a single syllable vill I utter."

"Okay," said Davis, "it's a deal."

Sunday came around, and Davis was sitting in the clubhouse when he happened to look up from his paper to see Goldberg standing in front of him, beaten and bloody.

"My God, Mr. Goldberg," he said, "how did this happen? I thought we had an agreement. No matter what happened, you weren't going to open your mouth."

"And zat agreement I kept," said Goldberg. "Not a void passed my lips, not a single syllable."

"So how did this happen?" asked Davis.

"I met mine foursome on the first hole, vhich is a par four. Not saying a void, not a syllable, I hit a nice tee shot. Mine second shot I put on the green. I two putted, and valked off to number two. Again a par four. I hit a lovely tee shot, vas on the green in two, two putted for par and valked over to number three—again not uttering a single void, not a syllable. Vee get to number three, vhich is the par three vit the vater hazard. I push mine tee shot, and it lands in the edge of the vater. As the four of us are valking up to the green together vee stopped to pick mine ball out of the vater. As I leaned over to pick up mine ball, the vater suddenly parted. They vere all over me in an instant!"

254

A foursome arrived one morning at one of the local golf courses. They went over to the starter's booth to see how long the wait would be to get out and play a round. One of the men went up to the starter and asked how long it would be to get out on the course.

"That's going to be a problem, sir," the starter told him. "We're all booked up for the entire day."

"There's nothing available at all?" asked the man.

"I'm very sorry, sir," he replied. "Nothing at all."

"Just out of curiosity," said the man, "let me ask you a question. If Nick Price, Greg Norman, Fred Couples, and Tom Kite showed up here right now, do you think you'd be able to get them out on the course right away?"

"I'm sure I would, sir," said the starter.

"Well, fine then," said the man. "Seeing as they're all playing at the U.S. Open this week, we'll just take their spots!"

255

First friend: "Have you heard about the miracle golf invention that can take unlimited strokes off of anybody's score instantly?"

Second friend: "No, I don't believe I have. What's it called?"

First friend: "An eraser!"

256

Alan takes his friend Bob out to the neighborhood executive course one day for a round on the links. Since this was Bob's first time playing the game, Alan took great pains to try and give his friend as much information as possible on the proper technique for swinging the club, but he also cautioned him that golf is a very difficult game and that he shouldn't expect too much from himself the first time out.

They arrive at the first hole and Alan hits a nice tee shot, putting the ball neatly on the green. Bob then gets up, hauls back, and blasts the ball skyward at the green. His ball hits, bounces once, and promptly rolls into the cup for a hole in one. Alan, standing there watching this has somewhat of a momentary mini-stroke, but, after a moment or two, pretty much manages to compose himself. He congratulates Bob and writes it off in his mind as some kind of beginner's luck.

They move on to the second hole where Alan again goes first. He hits another nice tee shot, once again putting the ball nicely on the green. He then steps aside to let Bob take a whack at it, assuming that now he'll get a taste of the *real* game. Bob once again steps up to his ball, brings the club back, and lets it fly. The ball sailed high into the sky, came down towards the green, and this time it didn't even bounce. It flew directly into the cup!

This time Alan goes directly into shock. No passing Go, no collecting two hundred dollars. He can't believe what he's just seen. Being a *real* golfer, his immediate instinct is to grab his good buddy by the throat and choke the life out of him, but, instead, he somehow manages to compose himself, take a deep breath and congratulates him once more, figuring that he just must be the luckiest S.O.B. on the face of the planet.

They then move on to the third hole. They arrive on the

third tee, and Alan decides that it's time for a change in the rotation, so he tells Bob to go ahead and hit first. Bob steps up to his ball and is about to hit. Suddenly, Alan can't take it anymore. He stops Bob in mid backswing.

"I don't get it," he said. "I've been playing this lousy game for more years than I care to remember and in all that time I've never once come close to getting a hole in one, and you, who've never so much as picked up a club before today, come out here and have the unmitigated gall to bang out two in a row. How in the world could that possibly happen?"

"I have no clue," said Bob. "I simply closed my eyes and swung the club. Let's see if I can do it again."

"Over my dead body!" cried Alan. "This time you have to keep your *eyes open!*"

257

John goes out to play some golf on a lovely weekend morning as a single. He arrives at the course and is paired with a couple—another man and a stunning woman. They exchange pleasantries, and the three of them head out on the course together. They're having a nice time chatting about this and that as they play. About the time they reach the fourteenth hole, the man looks at his watch, mumbles something about a business meeting of some kind, excuses himself, and walks off the course, leaving John and this lovely woman alone for the remainder of the round. They continue to have an enjoyable conversation as they play.

As they reach the eighteenth green, John finds his ball about two feet from the cup, while his new lady friend's is at least forty feet from the hole.

"You know what?" John says to her. "It's been so nice spending this time with you that if I make this putt, and it's okay with you, I'm going to take you out for the nicest lunch you ever had."

"That's most kind of you," says the lady. "I'd be delighted to join you for lunch."

John proceeds to step up and drain his ball right into the middle of the cup. He figures he's on the way to a nice lunch when the lady comes over to him.

"You know what?" she says. "Since you've been so kind to me, I'll tell you what *I'm* going to do. If I make *my* putt, forget lunch. If I make this putt, I'm going to take you to the nearest motel, and when I get you there, I'm going to make love to you all afternoon long like you've never had love made to you before."

Upon hearing this, John headed directly over to her ball and picked it up.

"That's a gimmee!"

258

Old Golfer to Young Golfer: "Remember, hope is an amazing thing."

Young Golfer to Old Golfer: "Why is that?"

Old Golfer to Young Golfer: "The first time I played golf I actually hit a decent shot. I've been playing for over forty years trying to do it again."

259

A husband and wife were on the ninth fairway at their club, about to hit their approach shots to the green, when all of a sudden from out of nowhere, a golf ball came whizzing past them, missing the husband by not more than a couple of inches. A minute or two later a woman comes over from the next fairway to retrieve her ball.

"Are you a crazy person?" said the wife. "You hit a lousy shot like that, and you don't have the courtesy or the brains to yell 'Fore.' You almost hit my husband."

"Gee," said the woman most apologetically, "I'm terribly sorry about that."

She then offered the wife her club.

"Here," she said. "Take a shot at mine."

260

An American tourist was overseas in Scotland and decided to stop by one of the local clubs for a round of golf. Being alone, he was paired with one of the local members. As they made their way down the twelfth fairway, the fellow noticed on the adjoining fairway a foursome who were all wearing black armbands.

"What's that all about?" inquired the American.

"Oh, that's Shamus' foursome," said his partner, taking off his cap and covering his heart. "Aye, it's a very sad thing, indeed. Shamus recently lost his golf ball."

261

A man goes to confession one day with something heavy on his mind. He goes into the confessional and sits down.

"How have you sinned, my son?" asks the priest.

"Oh, I've done a terrible thing, Father," groans the man. "I've used the Lord's name in vain."

"There, there, my son. It will be all right," says the priest. "Tell me how it happened."

"I was out playing golf the other day," the man began, "and for the first time in the thirty years that I've been playing the game, I actually had a chance to play a round at par. All I needed to do was to par the eighteenth hole."

"Golf can be a frustrating game, my son," said the priest. "Tell me what happened on the eighteenth."

"Well," continued the man, "I step up to the tee on eighteen and blast a gorgeous drive, smack down the middle of the fairway, but wouldn't you know it, the ball lands with a thud and plugs right into a huge divot that some kind soul hadn't bothered to replace."

"And that's when you used the Lord's name in vain?" asked the priest, a little anxiety creeping into his voice.

"No," said the man, "I wasn't going to let that stop me, not this time. I reached over to my bag and pulled out my five wood. I pulled the club back and hit down on the ball as hard as I could. It jumped out of the divot and sailed high into the air, right towards the green. But as fate would have it, just where it should have bounced on the fringe and run up to the hole, instead it hit off a sprinkler head just in front of the green and bounced clear over the green and into a sandtrap."

"And *that's* when you spoke the Lord's name in vain," said the priest, a little more anxiously.

"Actually, no, not then," he said as he continued. "I told you I was determined. I was not going to crumble in the face of adversity. I pulled out my trusty sand wedge. I took an open stance as I dug my feet into the sand, opened the club face up and swung for all I was worth. The ball arced high out of the trap, bounced once, and rolled straight as an arrow right towards the cup where it stopped just *six inches* from going in."

"*Jesus Christ,*" cried the priest, "*you missed the Goddamn putt!!!*"

262

Two friends ran into each other on the street one afternoon.

"I went to see the doctor today," the first fellow said.

"Oh, really," said the second. "What did he say?"

"Would you believe he said I can't play golf?"

"He's obviously been out with you before."

263

A man went into a local golf shop and bought a dozen balls. The clerk asked the man, "Would you like these wrapped?"

"No, thank you," said the man, "I'll just *drive* them home."

264

A frustrated golfer was complaining to his wife one evening over dinner.

"Honey," he said, "I really wish I could give up this rotten golf game of mine."

"Well for heaven's sake," she replied, "why don't you just grab the bull by the horns and just quit?"

"I can't," he said, "I've got too much money invested in sweaters!"

265

Three of the older club members were sitting together after an afternoon of nine holes discussing the current state of their golf games.

"I'll tell you," one of the gentlemen said to the others, "my golf game's not what it used to be. I used to be able to drive the ball 270, 280 yards on a good day, but now I consider myself lucky if I can hit it 210 or 220. I find it most distressing."

"Yes, I know what you mean," said another, "I definitely can't fade or draw the ball around those trees like I used to. Now I have to try to go over them to get to the green. What about you, Ed?"

Ed just let out a low groan.

"Any shot I can *find* makes me happy."

266

"Did you know that Shakespeare was a golfer?" one golfer asked his buddy.

"No," said his buddy, "I had no clue Shakespeare was a golfer."

"Well is happens to be true," he said. "I'm surprised you didn't know that. Aren't you familiar with one of his most famous lines?"

"I guess I'm not," said his friend. "What line is that?"

"You know the one," he said. "Haven't you ever heard, 'Putting is such sweet sorrow?'"

267

Wanting to give his young son some early exposure to golf, the father decided to take the four-year-old out on the links with him one morning. He figured it would be as good a time as any for the boy to have his first golfing experience, so Mommy packed them a goodie bag, and off they went to the course.

Several hours later, they returned home. The little boy came flying into the house with his father following behind. He found his mother in the living room and ran over to her yelling, "Mommy, we're home, we're home!"

"I can see you're home, sweetheart," said his Mom, giving him a great big hug and kiss. "How was your day with Daddy at the golf course?"

"It was *great*, Mommy. My Daddy must be the greatest golfer in the whole world," said the little one, beaming. "He hit that white ball all day long and hardly *ever* let it go into any of those little holes!"

268

Two hackers and a little old man are out on the golf course one day. They get to the par four eighth hole and one of the hackers hits first. He dubs his tee shot and sends it all of 125 yards down the fairway. The second hacker gets up and does the same thing as the first, sending his ball about 130 yards down the fairway. Next it's the little old man's turn. He gets up and hits what for him is a beautiful tee shot—right down the middle of the fairway, about 135 yards. They head off down the fairway and get to the first hackers ball. The hacker reaches down, pulls a clump of grass from the fairway, tosses it into the air, and turns to his caddie.

"Give me my four iron," he says, and takes the club and hits his shot.

Then they move over to the other hacker's ball. The second hacker reaches down, pulls a clump of grass from the fairway, and tosses it into the air.

"Give me my four iron," he says to his caddie. He takes the club and hits his shot.

Now they go over to the little old man's ball. When they get there, the little old man reaches down and pulls a clump of grass from the fairway and tosses it into the air. He then turns to his caddie.

"Give me my sweater."

269

Two friends were finishing up a particularly poor round of golf the other day. The first man complained to his friend.

"This is getting ridiculous. My game is going down the tubes. I can't take the stress of playing all this lousy golf. I think what I really need is a vacation."

"So, tell me," his friend asked, "where in the world can

you go on vacation and actually get *away* from golf?"

"I'm gonna go to the office!"

270

A low handicapper and a high handicapper were paired together at a local area competition. As they prepared to tee off on the first hole, the low handicapper turned to the high man.

"The way I see this competition shaping up, I can definitely see me having to shoot at least in the low seventies or maybe even break par to win. What do *you* think you'll have to shoot, in order to win?"

"What do I think *I'll* have to shoot here to win?" asked the hacker. "Most probably the *rest of the field!*"

271

An American and an English business associate were talking in a taxi going crosstown one day, when the subject of the conversation turned to golf.

"It would seem you Americans have managed to turn the grand old game of golf around backwards."

"What makes you say that?" asked the American.

"Why I should think it's quite obvious," stated the Englishman. "In the office, you talk of nothing but golf, and on the golf course you speak of nothing but business."

272

What's the definition of a lost ball?
A lost ball is a ball that's never been properly hit!

273

"I once tried to publish a book called *The Complete Book of Golf Terms*," a fellow confided to his friend.
"Were you successful?" his friend asked.
"No," he said, "it never had a chance."
"Why not?" his friend inquired.
"It was banned for indecency!"

274

A young man in his early thirties was paired for a round of golf one day with a man who was well into his seventies. The younger man was not entirely thrilled by this prospect, thinking the old gentleman would only slow down his game. Imagine his surprise and chagrin, when the older man proceeded to trash him by some fifteen strokes.

"Don't take it so hard, sonny," said the older man, trying to console the youngster. "You'll be burying me someday soon."

"Big deal," grumbled the young man to himself, as he walked off the eighteenth green. "It'll *still* be your hole!"

275

A man was brought into the emergency room of a major metropolitan hospital one day virtually at death's door. It seems that he had somehow gotten a golf ball lodged deep in his throat. The hospital personnel immediately rushed him into one of the operating rooms, where a dedicated team of surgeons and specialists went about the job of extracting the life-threatening orb. After many tense hours, the surgery was over, and the operation was a success. The patient was going to live. The chief doctor came out into the waiting room to find a man nervously pacing next to three ashtrays filled with cigarette butts.

"Are you a member of the family?" the doctor asked the man.

"No, Doc," replied the man. "It's my ball."

The sensitive woman golfer couldn't help herself. She had to go over to the sorrowful looking Scotsman she'd seen in the clubhouse wearing a black armband.

"Let me console you," she said.

"Och, lassie," said the Scotsman, "don't be telling me ye found me ball?"

The beginning golfer asked his caddie:
"What should I do with this divot?"
To which his caddie replied:

A) Why not take it home and practice on it?

B) Why don't you try growing vegetables on it?

C) Maybe you could have it declared the fifty-first state.

D) Why don't you bring it home, and use it as your own personal putting green?

E) Why don't you donate it to Brazil to help replace the rain forest?

F) Why not have it declared a national park?

G) You could always use it as a cover for Mount St. Helen's.

H) Why not donate it to the Jets or Giants for use as a practice field?

278

Wife to Husband: "How did your golf game go today, Dear?"

Husband to Wife: "Fine. I played with our dentist, Dr. Spiegel."

Wife back to Husband: "Oh, that's nice. How does he play?"

Husband back to Wife: "He plays well enough, except he has this annoying habit of continually walking over to the cup on each green and saying 'Would you open a little wider, please?'"

279

Arnie came home from his usual day at the golf course, went upstairs, showered, dressed and came downstairs for dinner. At the table, his wife asked him how his day had gone.

"Fine," was his response, and he continued, "but the

queerest thing happened. It had to do with the boy who was caddying for me—it was eerie. I kept having the feeling that I'd seen him somewhere before. He looked so familiar, but no matter how hard I tried, I just couldn't place him."

"That's it!" exclaimed his wife. "It's obvious that you've been playing far too much golf, and it's time you cut back and spent more time at home. That boy was *your son!*"

280

Jesus and St. Peter were out on the links one day. On this particular occasion, St. Peter was caddying for Jesus. They reached the sixth hole which was a 210-yard par three with a carry over a pond. Jesus turned to St. Peter, as they walked up to the tee.

"Give me my four iron." Jesus said.

Now, this request gave St. Peter quite a start.

"Your four iron?" he said incredulously. "You can't possibly carry the water with your four iron."

"Arnold Palmer would hit a four iron," said Jesus. "Give me my four iron."

"Okay," said St. Peter, "if that's what you want, but I'm telling you right here and now that if you put that ball into the water, there's no way I'm going to go in and get it for you."

With that said, Jesus took the four iron and hit a low line drive that flew about 180 yards and landed smack in the middle of the water.

After watching this, Jesus calmly turned to St. Peter.

"Go get me my ball."

"Go get me my ball!" cried St. Peter. "How could you ask me that? I told you, you'd never make it over the water and that I wasn't going to get your ball for you when you didn't. I pleaded with you. Why should I gave to get it?"

"Go and get me the ball, please," repeated Jesus.

"Fine!" said St. Peter as he stomped off down the fairway. "I'll get you your stupid ball."

He waded into the water, retrieved the ball, and slogged back to where Jesus was standing, dropping it at his feet.

"Are you happy now?" he asked.

"Yes, I am. Thank you," said Jesus. "Now give me my four iron."

"Your four iron!" gasped St. Peter, doing his level best to hold back a hemorrhage. "How in Heaven's name can you ask me for your four iron after what just happened?"

"Arnold Palmer would hit a four iron," said Jesus as he held out his hand.

"Here then, suit yourself," grumbled St. Peter, handing him the club, "but be forewarned. Under absolutely *no circum-*

stances whatsoever will I retrieve that ball for you if you hit it into the water."

"Not to worry," said Jesus.

This time he launched the ball high into the air only to see it come down again with a *plop* right in the middle of the water.

"Don't even *look* in my direction," snarled St. Peter.

"Hey, no problem-o," said Jesus as he headed towards the lake. Now, being Jesus and all, when he got to the pond, he simply walked across the water to the spot where his ball had gone in.

Just then, two other golfers in a cart who happened to be driving by witnessed this and stopped their cart by St. Peter.

"Say," they asked, "who does this guy think he is? Jesus Christ?"

"No," sighed St. Peter, "Arnold Palmer."

281

"I'm becoming a bit worried about my Uncle Louie," a fellow was commenting to his friend. "His cheating at golf is getting out of control."

"What makes you say that?" his friend asked.

"Well," said the man, "he's always taken some extra strokes

time and again, but now he's taking them on every hole he plays, and he can't control himself."

"How do you know that he can't control himself?"

"It became quite clear he had a problem the other day when I played with him," the man said. "He scored a hole in one and do you know what he put down on his scorecard?"

"No, what?" asked his friend.

"A zero!"

282

The club president came racing up to the first tee when he noticed one of the members about to commit a most grevious infraction of the rules of golf.

"Oh, sir...sir!" The president called out just as the member was beginning his backswing, causing him to jerk to a halt. "You're not allowed to tee off from there. You are a full three yards in front of the markers."

"Why don't you go and mind your own business," snapped the member. "This is my *third shot!*"

A few of the boys were sitting around the bar after a day of golfing when the subject of their conversation turned to what they considered to be the most difficult shot in golf.

"The most difficult shot in golf," began the first, "is, without question, the long iron out of the rough. The swing required to execute it properly makes it the hardest shot in golf."

"Nonsense," said the second, "the toughest shot in all of golf is the flop shot. It requires the most delicate touch and makes it far and away the hardest shot in golf."

"How could you say that?" the third guy chimed in. "There's absolutely no doubt about the most difficult shot in golf being the sand shot. One wrong move, and *BAM*...disaster! Nothing is as tough."

"You guys have no clue of what you speak," said the fourth guy. "I'll tell you about the toughest shot in golf. The toughest shot in golf is a five iron from 175 yards out that you slice so that it goes into a sand trap, hits a rock and bounces out, careens off a tree, bounces off a cart path, rolls up onto the green and into the hole. And before you say anything, I know for a fact that this is the most difficult shot in golf, because in the twenty-nine years I've been playing the game. I've only done it once!"

Mark called his friend Tom on the phone one evening to see how his golfing lessons were going.

"I don't think they're going too well," said Tom.

"What makes you say that?" asked Mark.

"Well, after six months of lessons I sat down with my pro for an evaluation," Tom continued.

"And what did he have to say?" asked Mark.

"He suggested that I take thirty days off," said Tom.

"Thirty days off?" said Mark. "Thirty days off and then do what?"

"Thirty days off," said Tom, "and then quit!"

A hack golfer gets himself an invitation to play at a ritzy country club where he gets a free caddie for the day. Being the hacker he is, he plays terribly all day. As he gets to the eighteenth hole, he notices a lake off to the left of the fairway. He looks over at his caddie.

"That's it!" he says. "I've played like crap all day, and I can't take it anymore. I'm going over to that lake, and I'm going to drown myself."

Hearing this, the caddie just looks back at him.

"You're welcome to try, sir, but I don't think you'll be able to keep your head down long enough."

286

A Scotsman gets shipwrecked and washed ashore on a small island. When he wakes up on the beach, he sees a beautiful girl standing over him.

"Would you like some food?" she says to him.

"Och, lassie," the Scot croaks hoarsely, "I havna' ittin a bite in a week noo and I'm a verra hungry."

She disappears into the woods and reappears a few moments later with a heaping helping of Haggis (a Scottish delicacy about which the less said, the better).

After he chokes it down she asks, "Would you be wanting anything to drink?"

"Och, aye!" he says. "The Haggis has made me verra thirsty and I wad verra much like somethin to drink."

She goes off into the woods again and this time comes back with a bottle of 75-year-old single malt scotch whiskey. By now, the Scotsman is starting to think that he's died and gone to Heaven when the girl leans close to him and whispers into his ear, "Would you like to play around?"

"Och, lassie!" he exclaims. "Don't be tellin me ye've got a golf course here too!"

287

A man belongs to a private golf club where the fourteenth hole is a long par three with a carry over water. The guy's a decent player, but no matter how good a round he has going, whenever he gets to the fourteenth, no matter what he tries, he always puts his ball in the water.

One day he's playing with his usual foursome and they get to the fourteenth and sure enough, he hits his ball into the water. By now he's beside himself and just doesn't know what to do, when one of his friends decides to offer some advice.

"You know," he says, "you've tried everything else. Why not try praying to God. At this point, you've got nothing to lose."

So the next weekend, the guy goes to church, and he prays with all his heart and soul.

"Oh, God, if you're listening, I need an answer to my problem."

Suddenly, much to his amazement, he hears the voice of God.

"Go to your golf course next week and listen for my voice. You shall receive the answer you seek."

Next week comes, and he's out on the course, and sure enough, just as he's about to tee off on the fourteenth, he once again hears the voice of God.

"Go to your golf bag," the voice orders him.

He goes over to his bag.

"Take out your five wood."

He takes out his five wood.

"Go back to your bag," the voice commands.

He goes back to his bag.

"Take out a ball."

He takes out a new ball.

"No, schmuck, an old ball!"

288

A few of the guys are talking in the grillroom one day after a round of golf, and one of them is commenting on how he sometimes takes his dog with him when he goes out to play.

"Whenever I get a bogey, my dog does a backflip," the man says.

"Really?" said the others.

"And when I get a double bogey, he does *two* backflips."

"That's amazing!" they said. "How does he do it?"

"Easy,"he said. "I kick him *twice!*"

289

A fellow is out of town on business for a few days and decides to stop by a local course to play a round of golf. He gets to the club and heads over to the caddie shack, where he's informed by the caddie master that, unfortunately, there are no caddies presently available.

"However," said the caddie master, "if you would be interested, we do have a mechanical caddie that could be at your disposal."

The fellow thought this a little strange, but, being a curious type, he figured what the heck. So he told the caddie master he'd give the mechanical caddie a try. The caddie master disappeared into the back room and emerged a few moments later followed by a polished stainless steel mechanical man. The robot grabbed his clubs, and off they went.

Well, to say that this fellow played the round of his life is the understatement of the year. When the round was finished and they returned to the caddie shack, he couldn't stop raving about the mechanical man.

"It was the most incredible thing I've ever experienced," he said. "All the yardages he gave me were perfect to the inch. Every club he handed me was exactly the right club for the situation. He gave me so many swing tips, by the end of the round, he had me looking like Bobby Jones, for God's sake."

"I'm glad you were pleased, sir," replied the caddie master. "It's unfortunate we're going to have to cancel the program."

"Cancel the program!" exclaimed the shocked man. "Why would you have to do that?"

"As you are aware," said the caddie master, "the caddies are made of metal, and, while you were out on the course, we received a number of complaints from other players about the sun reflecting off him and making it difficult for them to play."

The fellow thought about this for a moment.

"I have an idea," he said to the caddie master. "Why not just put uniforms on them? That should solve the problem."

"We tried that once before," said the caddie master. "The very next day they formed a union...and went on strike!"

290

A foursome is teeing off on the first hole when one of the men looks at the guy about to tee off and notices something.

"That's an interesting looking ball you've got there," he said. "What kind is it?"

"Oh, it's absolutely the latest in ball technology," the guy answered. "It's made of special space-age composite material so that it always seeks out the cup. It's got a built-in beeper that goes off when it lands, and it also has a built-in light that automatically goes on when the sun goes down."

"That's amazing!" said his friend. "Where did you get it?"

"I found it."

291

Sam joins a new golf club, and the first day out, he's paired with three men who play together every week. Upon hearing this, Sam asks if they'd mind if he became the fourth for their regular game. The man said there was no problem with that and that they'd be delighted to have him.

They played their round, and Sam played righty. The next week, however, was different. Sam played lefty. The third week came along, and Sam played righty again. Now it was the fourth week that came along, and before the foursome teed off, they pulled Sam off to the side.

"We're curious," said one of the men. "The first week we

played together, you played righty, the second week you played lefty, and last week you played righty again. What's the deal?"

"Oh that," said Sam. "it's really quite simple. I play from whatever side my wife sleeps on the night before. If she sleeps on her right side, I play righty. If she sleeps on her left side, I play lefty."

"That makes sense, I guess," said one of the others, "but what happens if she sleeps on her back?"

"It means I'll be fifteen minutes late!"

292

Two strangers are paired together for a round of golf at a local course. They reach the first green, and the first guy, being away, gets ready to putt. Just as he's about to hit the ball, the guy he's playing with suddenly starts rocking from side to side.

"Excuse me," he says, lifting up from his shot, "I'm trying to putt if you don't mind."

That said, he takes his shot, misses, and walks off the green mumbling to himself.

Comes the second hole and the fellow's about to putt when, once again, this guy starts rocking from side to side.

"Pardon me," he grumbles, "I'm trying to putt!"

The guy stops rocking, but of course the fellow misses his putt, and this time walks off the green more than a bit ticked off.

They arrive at the third green, and, once again, the first guy is away. Sure enough, just as he's about to putt the ball, the other guy starts rocking from side to side.

"Dammit!" he explodes, now thoroughly aggravated. "I'm trying to play golf here. Why do you keep rocking side to side like that?"

"I'm so sorry," the guys says. "I'm a sailor on leave from my ship for the first time in three months, and I haven't gotten my land legs yet. I can't help rocking from side to side."

The first guy just glared back at him.

"Look, bud," he snapped, "I don't care what your problem is. I happen to be a lawyer, and you don't see me running around here trying to screw everybody."

293

Dave and Al tee off on the ninth hole of their home course, which happens to run parallel to a main road. They reach their tee shots on the fairway, and Dave's about to hit his second when they look up to see a funeral procession passing by. Dave stops his preparations and puts his club down on the ground. He then turns around, faces the road, takes off his hat, covers his heart and bows his head.

Al looks at him in bewilderment.

"Why in the world are you doing that?" he asks.

Dave looks up.

"After thirty-five years of marriage, it's the least I can do for my wife."

294

A rabbi and a priest are out on the golf course one day. Unfortunately, the rabbi isn't having a very good round. As a matter of fact, he's having a lousy round. And to top it off, every time he hits a crummy shot he proceeds to curse up a storm, which is really starting to upset the priest.

"Rabbi," says the priest, "it's really not right for a man such as yourself to use this kind of language. If you do not stop it, I fear the Lord will strike you down."

The rabbi pays basically no attention to the priest, and they go on with their round, with the rabbi continuing to curse like there's no tomorrow. They finally reach the eighteenth tee and the rabbi slices his tee shot off into the woods, which causes him to launch into a veritable torrent of obscenities.

Suddenly, from out of nowhere, the sky becomes pitch black, and the winds begin to howl.

"See!" cries the priest. "I told you this would happen."

The two men are frozen in their tracks with fear when from out of the center of the storm, a huge lightning bolt descends from the heavens, striking the priest and instantly reducing him to a smoking pile of ashes. The rabbi just stands there quaking in his golf shoes when suddenly a booming voice from the heavens cries out,

"Dammit . . . I missed!"

295

The newlywed couple was away on their honeymoon. The first night in their hotel suite they were cuddled up in bed together when the new husband turned to his bride.

"Sweetheart," he said, "now that we're married, I have a confession to make."

"What is it, Pookie?" she asked.

"I'm an avid golfer," he said. "Chances are you won't see much of me on the weekends."

"That's okay, my darling," she purred, "But as long as we're at it, I, too, have a confession to make."

"What's that, my pet?" he asked.

"I'm a hooker."

"That's no problem, my lambkin," he replied. "All you need to do is remember to drop your left shoulder and follow through on your swing."

296

Definition of a Mulligan: "The chance to immediately repeat a mistake."

297

What's the *real* reason your golf pro always tells you to keep your head down?

So you can't see him laughing at you!

298

Two women were talking the other day over tea.

"Did I tell you that my husband has taken up golf?" the first lady asked her friend.

"No, as a matter of fact, you didn't," her friend replied, "How's he doing?"

"Evidently, very well," said the first lady. "He's only played three times, but his friends tell me that he's already throwing his clubs as far as men who've been playing the game for years!"

299

Two little bugs were crossing a fairway on a golf course one sunny day when they came across a golf ball. Just as they were about to continue around the ball, they felt the ground under them begin to shake. Panic spread across their faces, as they looked up to see the golfer approaching. Fearing for their very lives, one bug turned to the other.

"Oh my," he cried, "we're going to be crushed! I don't want to die. What are we going to do?"

"We need to find a safe place where we won't get hit," said the other bug. "Quick! Climb up on the ball!"

300

Ancient golfing truism: Old golfers never die...they just lose distance!

301

First friend: "I played golf the other day with a group of guys who were so old...

Second friend: "How old were they?"

First friend: "They were so old that when I talked about grip, they thought I was talking about dentures!"

302

First guy: "Have you heard about the new golf ball that's made out of sodium bicarbonate?"

Second guy: "No, I don't believe I have."

First guy: "It's pretty neat. If you hit it into a lake, all you have to do to find it is to walk down to the edge of the water, and wait for the fish that swallowed it to belch!"

303

The general contractor for the golf club was meeting at the clubhouse with the chairwoman of the members' advisory board to discuss the colors to be used for the recently approved repainting of the clubhouse.

They went into the first room, which the chairwoman told him was to be painted blue. With that, he took out his notepad and made a notation. He then walked over to a nearby window, opened it up and shouted, *"Green side up!"* They then walked into the second room, which the chairwoman informed him was to be painted white. He again took out his pad, made a notation, walked over to the nearest window, opened it up and shouted, *"Green side up."*

By now the chairwoman was starting to get curious, but she said nothing. They walked into the third room, which she informed him will be painted yellow. Just like the last two times, the contractor makes a note in his pad and starts to head over to the window.

"Forgive me for asking," she said to him, "but why on earth do you keep going over to the window and yelling 'Green side up'?"

"I'm terribly sorry about that, ma'am," he replied, "but I have a crew of *blonds* laying sod on the first tee."

THE OFFICIAL RULES OF BEDROOM GOLF

1. Each player shall furnish his own equipment, usually one club and two balls.

2. Any and all play on a course must be approved by the owner of the hole.

3. Unlike outdoor golf, the object of bedroom golf is to get the club into the hole and keep the balls out.

4. For the most effective play, the club should have a firm shaft. (Note: Course owners are permitted to check shaft thickness before play begins.)

5. Course owner reserves the right to restrict club length and thickness to avoid damage to the hole.

6. The object of the game is to take as many strokes as necessary until the course is satisfied that play is complete. Failure to do so may result in being denied the right to play the course again.

7. It is considered very bad form to begin playing the hole immediately upon arrival at the course. The experienced, con-

siderate player will take the time to admire the entire course, with special attention being paid to well-formed bunkers.

8. Players are cautioned not to mention other courses they have played, or are currently playing, to the course owner. Upset course owners have been known to severely damage a player's equipment for such a breach of etiquette.

9. Players are always encouraged to have proper rain gear along for protection, just in case.

10. Players should assure themselves that their match is scheduled properly, particularly when a new course is being played for the first time. Previous players have been known to become irate if they discover someone else playing what they considered to be a private course.

11. Players should not assume that a course is in shape for play at all times. Some players may be embarrassed if they find the course to be temporarily under repair. Players are advised to be extremely tactful in this situation. Most advanced players will find alternate means of play when this is the case.

12. Players are strongly advised to obtain the course owner's permission before attempting to play the back nine.

13. Slow play is encouraged; however, players should be prepared to proceed at a quicker pace at the owner's request.

14. It is considered outstanding performance, time permitting, to play the course several times in one match.

15. The course owner shall be the sole judge of who is the best player.

Players are advised to think twice before considering permanent membership at a given course. Additional assessments may be levied by the course owner at any time, and all the rules are subject to uncontested change. For these reasons, many players prefer to play several different courses.

305

Old Ned was an avid golfer all his life. Unfortunately, as he got into his sixties his eyesight started to fail him. He didn't want to give up the game he loved, so he went to the family eye doctor to see if there was anything that could be done. The doctor said there wasn't really anything he could do about his vision, but he had an idea. He knew a man named Jack who was ninety-seven years old and still had perfect vision. "Eyes of an eagle" was how the doctor described him.

"I know that Jack's been looking to get out more," said the

doctor. "Maybe you could take him out golfing with you, and you could use him to watch where you hit your ball."

Ned was having a bit of trouble believing the doctor. A guy almost one hundred years old with the eyes of an eagle is a little hard to swallow, but, at that point, he didn't have many options, so he called up Jack (who, incidentally, was thrilled to have a chance to get out of the house) and made arrangements to bring him golfing with him.

The day came, and they arrived at the golf course. They got up on the first tee and Ned positions Jack so that he can see the whole fairway. Ned then steps up to the tee and drives his ball. It felt like a good hit, but Ned couldn't see where it went, so he turned to Jack.

"Did you see my shot?" he asked Jack.

"Sure did," said Jack. "Clear as a bell."

"That's great!" said Ned. "Where did it go?"

"I don't know," said Jack.

"What do you mean, you don't know?" asked an incredulous Ned. "I thought you said you saw it clear as a bell."

"I did see it clear as a bell," said Jack.

"Then how come you don't know where it is?" Ned snapped.

"I forgot."

306

A few of the guys were discussing golf history in the grillroom one afternoon.

"I bet I know something about golf history that you don't know," one of the fellows said to his friends.

"And what would that be?" they asked.

"I happen to know that Samson was the world's first golfing addict."

"What are you talking about?" they asked. "How was Samson a golfing addict?"

"Simple," he said, "even with all his great strength, he couldn't break away from the links!"

307

A foreign professor who was teaching accounting at an American university was invited by a member of the school's golf team to come out and play golf for the first time. They arrived at the course, and the professor turned to the student.

"What do I do?" he asked.

"You have to hit the ball towards the flag over there on the green," the student told him.

The professor teed up his ball and proceeded to smack that sucker straight down the fairway. The ball rolled onto the green where it came to a stop less than an inch from the hole.

"What do I do now?" he asked the stunned student.

"You're supposed to hit the ball into the cup," he said.

"Oh, great!" exclaimed the professor. *"Now* you tell me!"

308

Who's the biggest money loser in golf?
Anyone playing his boss.

309

Who's the biggest money winner in golf?
The boss.

310

A real jerk of a guy goes out to play a round of golf with a few friends one day. Right before he's about to tee off on the first hole, a kindly looking fellow walks up to him on the tee and hands him a card. The card reads:

"Hello, I am a deaf mute, and I am playing alone. I was wondering, if it would cause you no inconvenience, if you'd mind if I played through?"

Well, what does the jerk do? He takes the card and throws it right back in the poor guy's face.

"No way, you little creep," he says. "I got here first, and I'm going to tee off first. You'll just have to wait your turn like the rest of us, and if you don't like it, you can take a flying leap."

"Do you really want to be like that?" his friends asked.

"You bet your buns," said the jerk. "Screw him!"

So with that, the jerk tees off and hits a nice drive down the fairway. His friends then hit, and they and their caddies head off down the fairway to their balls. The jerk reaches his ball, picks out an iron, checks the placement of the flag, and addresses the ball. Suddenly, he gets nailed in the back of the head by a flying golf ball, knocking him flat on his face. He jumps to his feet rubbing his head and screaming like a madman.

"What the... why that little son of a gun hit me," he said, as he turned back in the direction of the tee. "I'm going to kill him!"

Then he turned to his caddie.

"Now what's he doing?"

"He's holding up four fingers."

311

Golfer to caddie: "I'd move heaven and earth to be able to break 100!"

Caddie to golfer: "You might want to try heaven. You've already moved most of the earth."

312

Golfer to partner: "I'm anxious to make this shot. That's my mother-in-law up there on the clubhouse porch."

Partner to golfer: "Don't be ridiculous. It's well over 300 yards. You couldn't possibly hit her from here."

313

A man who was a total golf nut was married to a woman who lived only to attend auction sales. It seemed they both had the habit of talking in their sleep. One night, the husband must have been dreaming of being out on the links because at one point, he rolled over and yelled, "Fore!"

It obviously somehow got through to his wife, because she then rolled over towards him and shouted, "Four twenty-five!"

314

Why did the golfer bring two pair of pants with him to the golf course?

Because he had a hole-in-one! (*Ouch*)

315

Two new mothers were talking one day about what they wanted their children to be when they grew up.

"It really doesn't matter to me what my children become," said the first mother, "as long as they're happy."

"I want my son to be happy," said the second mother, "but I've already made sure that he'll grow up to be a doctor."

"He's only six months old," said the first mom. "How can you be sure that he'll grow up to be a doctor?"

"Simple," said the second mom. "I just went out and bought him his first set of golf clubs!"

316

John had just about given up hope of ever finding the perfect woman. He loved the game of golf, and since he could never seem to find a woman who shared his love and knowledge of the game, he figured it was just going to be his lot in life to remain alone.

As fate would have it, one evening after playing a round at his club, he decided to join a few friends for drinks at the local après golf tavern. Upon entering the establishment, his eyes were immediately drawn to an absolutely stunning woman standing by the bar talking with some people. He had to meet her. Throwing caution to the wind, he somehow, during the course of the evening, managed to make his way over to the bar and to strike up a conversation with her.

They started talking and really seemed to hit it off. The next thing they knew, it had gotten late and the bar was about to close.

"I've never done this before," she said as she gazed into his eyes, "but would you like to come home with me?"

"I find you *very* attractive, and we're getting along great," he replied. "I *really* do want to go home with you, but to tell you the truth, I'm scared. You see, I'm a golfer, and I always seem to find myself in relationships with women who aren't. Things never work out, and I end up getting hurt. I don't know if I can go through that again."

"I don't think that will be a problem this time," she cooed.

"How do you know that?" John asked.

"Let me put it to you this way," she said pressing her supple body up against the length of his and whispering in his ear. "Is that an extra long, very stiff shafted, graphite/boron composite, oversized titanium headed driver in your pocket...or are you just happy to see me?"

317

First golfer: "I played golf the other day with a guy who hit the ball soooo far."

Second golfer: "How far?"

First golfer: "He hit the ball so far, that when we got to the yardage marker by his ball, the marker said 'YOU DA MAN!'"

318

"I'm sick and tired of being left alone every weekend while you go out and play golf," grumbled the golf widow to her husband one morning over breakfast. "If you think you're going to play today, you've got another think coming!"

"Don't be ridiculous," replied her husband. "Believe me when I tell you that golf is absolutely the furthest thing from my mind. Now, can we please end this silly discussion once and for all. Oh, and would you mind passing me the putter?"

A businessman joined a swanky country club, although he knew absolutely nothing about the game of golf. His first time out on the course his caddie handed him a driver at the first tee, but the man refused and demanded a putter. The caddie protested that he'd never make the 425-yard-long hole with a putter, but the fellow insisted and, much to the caddie's amazement, slammed the ball some 240 yards.

For his second shot, he refused his caddie's suggestion of a four iron and instead pulled out a pitching wedge over his caddie's objections and blasted a shot, somehow getting the ball on the green.

Then to sink his putt, he looked over to his caddie.

"Give me my driver," he said.

Upon hearing this, the caddie almost had a coronary. He argued vehemently against using the driver, but it was in vain. The man threatened to fire him on the spot if he didn't give him the club. The caddie handed him the club, and wouldn't you know, he sunk the putt.

"Okay Mister Know-It-All," said the man to the caddie, "now's your chance. What club do I use to get it out?"

A primate researcher and his friend were out on the golf course one day discussing his latest project.

"We just acquired a mountain gorilla at the institute," he told his friend, "and the first thing we did was to teach him how to play golf."

"That's amazing," said his friend. "How does he play?"

"We took him out on the course the other day," said the researcher, "handed him the driver on the first tee, and watched as he proceeded to hit the ball over 450 yards landing it smack on the green of the long par four, all of three inches from the hole. We got to the green and handed him the putter."

"Don't tell me he sank the putt?" said his friend.

"Not exactly. Although he did hit the ball," sighed the researcher, "four hundred fifty yards!"

What's the difference between learning to drive a car and learning to play golf?

With one you hit everything and with the other you hit nothing.

322

First golfer: "Hey, I don't like the way you've been cheating out here."

Second golfer: "If you know a better way, I'm certainly open to it!"

323

Husband to wife: "What do you think would go well with my new golfing ensemble?"

Wife to Husband: "How about a nice set of waders?"

324

A fellow is out on the golf course one day, and he's not having a very good round. After watching his agony for a few hours, his caddie finally can't take it anymore.

"Pardon me, sir," he says. "If I might make a suggestion. It appears to me that you're not addressing the ball properly."

"Forget it!" snaps the man, picking up his ball and throwing it into the woods. "I was polite to it for as long as I could!"

John was an extremely avid golfer but frankly, he was also a smug, self-centered, cynical son of a gun, so it came as no surprise that when he passed away, few tears were shed.

Anyway, John shows up at the Pearly Gates where St. Peter is waiting for him. Rather than just passing through the gates like a normal person who is given the opportunity to enter Heaven would do, John has to stop to ask a question.

"St. Peter," he says, "before I agree to come in, I want to know exactly what kind of golf course you have here."

"That should not matter to you, my son," said St. Peter.

"But it does matter to me," replied John in a tone of voice that if he had any brains at all, he would have left behind on Earth, "and if I can't see it then I'm not coming in!"

"Very well, my son," said St. Peter, "as you wish. Look through the gates."

John leaned forward and looked through the gates. What he saw almost made him sick to his stomach. It was the probably the shabbiest, most rundown, poorest looking excuse for a golf course he had ever had the misfortune of seeing.

"Forget it!" he snapped at St. Peter. "There's no way in Hell I'm going to spend all of eternity playing on that course!"

Just then John hears another voice calling to him from behind. It was the Devil calling him over to his gate.

"Come over and see what I have to offer you," he says.

John goes over to the gate and peers through. His eyes widen as he beholds absolutely the most fabulous golf course that he could ever begin to imagine.

Seeing this thing of beauty, he turns to the Devil.

"I want to play *that* course," he says.

"All you need to do is step through the gates and it's yours forever," said the Devil.

And step through them he did, paying no attention to the sound of St. Peter's voice pleading with him not to go in. The gates closed behind him...and it was done.

John never felt such excitement as he walked up to the first tee and beheld the magnificence that was laid out before him.

"I can't wait another second," he said to the Devil. "I have to play *right now!* Where are my clubs and ball?"

The Devil just looked at him and began to laugh.

"What's so funny?" John asked the Devil.

"There aren't any!"

326

Four guys tee off on the par four twelfth hole at their golf club. The hole requires a 180-yard carry over a deep ravine. Three of the four lay up short of the ravine. The fourth guy tries to clear it, but comes up short and watches as his ball vanishes over the edge. So down he goes to find his ball, while the other three wait for him on the other side. They're standing there waiting for him for a few minutes when his ball finally pops out, and rolls down the fairway. Their friend emerges from the ravine, and one of the others asks him how many shots it took to get himself out.

"I got out in *one!*" he states.

"Nonsense!" they exclaim. "We distinctly heard you take six swings when you were in there. How do you explain that?"

"Easy," he said, "echoes!"

327

Two friends passed each other in between holes on the golf course one weekend. After they exchanged their initial pleasantries, the first fellow asked his friend what he shot. The guy just looked at him rather dejectedly.

"I shot a seventy-two," he sighed.

"Why so glum?" inquired his friend. "A seventy-two is a great score."

"Not for the first hole, it's not!"

328

Once upon a time, there was a golfer who became shipwrecked all alone on a desert island. Being a resourceful type of guy, as well as having quite a bit of time on his hands, this fellow managed to fashion himself a lovely little nine-hole golf course to play right there on the island. He was really quite clever. He used driftwood for markers. He fashioned himself a set of clubs, using old fish bones, and he made balls out of coral.

One day, as fate would have it, another man became shipwrecked and washed up on the same island as this guy. Taking the newcomer on a tour of the island, he was most anxious to show him the golf course he had put together and to get his opinion of it.

"So," he asked, "what do you think my course?"

"Oh, I suppose it's okay," replied the man.

"Okay!" said the shocked golfer. "Just okay? why, just look at the water hazard alone!"

329

If an employee and his boss are playing golf, how can you tell who's who?

The employee is the one who gets a hole in one and says, *"OOPS!"*

330

A naive new golfer is on the tee at one of the course's par three holes. Having more bravado than talent, he swears to his playing companions that he's going to hole out in two shots. That said, he tees his ball up and proceeds to dribble the ball about fifteen yards down the fairway.

Embarrassed, he turns to his fellow players.

"Looks like it's time for one *heck* of a putt!"

331

Two men were in the clubhouse the other day discussing their respective golf games.

"I played golf with my boss the other day," the first guy said. "At the very first hole, he got up and topped his tee shot. It rolled all of about fifty yards down the fairway leaving him almost 385 yards to the hole."

"What did you do?" asked his friend.

"It was a no-brainer," he said. "I conceded the putt!"

332

An amateur was playing at a local pro-am and was paired with a touring pro. At the end of the round, as the amateur was saying good-bye to the pro and thanking him for the day, he felt the need to ask the pro what he thought about his game.

"It's pretty good," said the pro, "but I still prefer golf."

333

Two heavyset friends took up golf under doctor's orders because they needed the exercise. They went out to the course and prepared to tee off on their first round.

"I'm not in very good shape and I know next to nothing about golf," said the first fellow. "I don't think I'll be able to play for very long."

"I'm not in shape either and I probably know less about golf than you, so I'll tell you what" said the second. "We'll just play until one of us gets a hole in one."

334

Having taken almost four hours just to play the front nine, the hacker turned to his caddie.

"You must be tired of carrying that bag," he said.

"No, sir," replied the caddie, "just of counting!"

335

Wife to frustrated Husband: "If you hate the game so much, why do you continue to play?"

Husband back to Wife: "You just don't understand. It's not *the* game. It's *my* game!"

336

With the prices they get for a round of golf and the cost of equipment these days, it's not just the clubs that are getting shafted!

337

After completing a particularly crummy round of golf, the hacker asked his playing partner,

"What do you think I should give my caddie?"
Came the response.
"How about your clubs?"

Bob came home from the golf course the other day in a terrible mood.

"What's the matter with you?" asked his wife.

"It's that son of a gun, Jim," complained Bob. "I'm never going to play golf with him again! He's the biggest cheater in the world."

"Why do you say that?" she asked.

"I'll tell you why," he said. "We were all tied up in our match going to the eighteenth hole. We walk up to the eighteenth green and that miserable so and so finds his ball sitting *twelve inches* from the cup. I could have *screamed!*"

"So what's the big deal?" she asked. "That's possible."

"No it's not!" cried Bob, "Not when his ball was *in my pocket!*"

339

A foursome is on the green of a par-three hole when a ball comes rolling up and stops six inches from the cup. Thinking they'll have a little fun, one of them gently nudges the ball with his foot into the hole.

A few moments later, a guy comes walking up to the green asking if anyone had seen his ball. With little smirks on their faces, they gesture to the cup.

The guy gets all excited, runs over to the cup, picks out his ball, and turns to yell back to his playing partners.

"Hey guys, look," he shouts, "I got a twelve!"

340

Harry and Rose had been married for over forty years. They're out on the golf course one day, at the first tee. Harry's about to tee off when, suddenly, Rose shouts out.

"Harry!"

Harry pays no attention to her, takes his tee shot and then turns around to her.

"What?"

"If I were to die before you," she asks, "would you remarry?"

"Of course I would," said Harry. "You wouldn't want me to spend the rest of my life alone, would you?"

And they continue on.

A couple of holes later, just as Harry is about to tee off, Rose again calls out.

"Harry!"

Again he ignores her, takes his tee shot and then turns around.

"What?"

"If you remarry," she asks him, "are you going to bring this woman into our house?"

"Why not?" replies Harry. "The house is already paid for. It wouldn't make sense not to."

And they continue on.

A couple of holes later, again as Harry is about to tee off, Rose blurts out.

"Harry!"

Harry once again pays her no never mind, hits his tee shot and then turns around.

"What?"

"This woman," says Rose, "are you going to take her into our bed?"

"I would think so," says Harry. "Where else would you want me to put her?"

And they continue on.

Sure enough, a few holes later, just as Harry's about to tee off, Rose once again calls out.

"Harry!"

As usual, Harry ignores her, takes his tee shot and then turns around.

"What?"

"Are you going to let this woman use my golf clubs?"

"Of course not!" says Harry. "She's a *lefty!*"

341

A doctor, an architect, and a lawyer were eating their lunch one day at the golf club when the conversation turned to their respective dogs, who according to each of them were quite extraordinary.

They decided to bet on who had the most intelligent dog. The doctor offered to show his dog first and turned to the parking lot and called out.

"Hippocrates, come!"

Hippocrates came running in, and the doctor told him to do his stuff. Hippocrates ran out onto the golf course, sniffed around for a moment, and then proceeded to dig up a pile of human bones. He dragged the bones into the club and assembled them into a complete, fully articulated human skeleton. The doctor patted Hippocrates on the head and gave him a cookie.

The architect was hardly impressed and called out for his dog.

"Sliderule, come!"

Sliderule ran into the room, and the architect told him to do his thing. Sliderule immediately chewed the skeleton to pieces and then reassembled the fragments into an unbelievably detailed model of the Taj Mahal. The architect patted his dog on the head and gave him a cookie.

The lawyer just sat back and called out.

"B.S., come!"

B.S. came flying into the room and without so much as a word from the lawyer, immediately ran over to the other two dogs, stole their cookies, auctioned off the replica of the Taj Mahal to the other members of the club for a huge fee, and then went outside and played a round of golf.

342

First golfer: "That Sam must be the grouchiest golfer I've ever had the misfortune to tee up a ball with."

Second golfer: "Why do you say that?"

First golfer: "I played golf with him last week, and he was so grouchy that he made a hole in one on the third hole and he actually complained that now he wasn't going to get the putting practice he wanted."

343

First Woman: "How was your husband's golf game?"
Second Woman: "Not very good, I think."
First Woman: "Well, didn't you ask him?"
Second Woman: "No, I know better. He came home with twigs in his hair."

344

Q: What goes "Putt, putt, damn...putt, putt, damn...putt, putt, damn?"
A: A lousy golfer.

345

Scene: Woman bragging to her friend.
"My son is such a good golfer, he was just offered a scholarship to medical school."

346

Two old guys were talking in the clubhouse one day.

"You know what the problem with this game is?" the first guy asked.

"No, what?" asked the second guy.

"Now that I finally have enough money for new balls, I can't hit 'em far enough to lose 'em."

347

The husband stormed into the house and threw his golf clubs down the basement stairs.

"What's the matter with you?" his wife asked.

"I can't take it anymore," he screamed. "I can't even break 100 by *cheating!*"

348

Having forgotten which golf course the boys were sneaking off to that day, a fellow calls his friend's office. His secretary picks up the phone.

"Oh, he's away from his desk right now," she said.

"I already know that," said the friend. "What I need to know is, is he ten miles away from his desk, or twenty?"

349

Larry wasn't paying attention as his friend walked up to the tee. He heard his practice swing and turned to see him standing almost directly over his ball.

"Maybe you're standing too close to the ball," he said to his buddy.

His friend glared at him.

"I just hit it."

350

Two members of the local club ran into each other in town.

"Did you hear what happened?" said the first man. "It was the talk of the clubhouse."

"No, I didn't. What happened?" said the second man.

"It seems that two golfers were out on the course discussing their scores, and one of them actually told the truth!"

"You're kidding!" said the second man, stunned. "What did he say?"

"He called the other guy a liar!"

Q: What are the first three things an old golfer loses?
A: Distance, accuracy, and uh,...

A guy comes home from playing golf one day, beaten to a pulp. His wife sees him and goes into shock.

"My God!" she exclaimed. "What happened to you?"

"I learned something today," he groaned.

"What on earth did you learn?" his wife asked.

"I learned that when a guy gets stuck in a bunker, you don't stand next to him and count strokes."

Her husband came home from playing golf and dropped dejectedly into a chair.

"How bad?" his wife asked.

"How bad?" he said. "I'll tell you how bad. I played so badly that when I went to post my score, the only thing that would come up on the computer screen was *'You shot a what?!'*"

354

"I just got back from a week at a great resort," a fellow told his friend. "They had six different golf courses."

"That sounds great," his friend replied. "But how did you decide which one to play?"

"Oh, it was easy," he said. "I'd just go out in the morning to the nearest tee and hit a ball. Wherever it landed, that was the course I'd play."

355

Two old friends met at the golf course.

"How's it going?" asked the first guy.

"Not so good," said the second. "My wife's divorcing me."

"Why, that's terrible," said the first. "What happened?"

"I made a five and a half footer on the eighteenth green," he replied.

"So what's wrong with making a putt?" the first guy asked.

"It wasn't a putt," he said. "It was a brunette."

356

A golfer drove his tee shot way out of bounds and into a farmer's chicken coop killing his prize hen. After locating the farmer, the golfer expressed his remorse.

"I'm so sorry," the man said. "Please let me replace her."

"Not so fast," said the farmer. "Just how many eggs can you lay a day?"

357

Two women met at the golf club.

"My," said the first woman, "isn't that a new golf bag and set of clubs you have there?"

"It sure is," said the second woman. "I caught my husband fooling around with our maid."

"Why, that's terrible," said the first. "You fired her, of course?"

"Certainly not," said the second woman. "I'm holding out for a brand new cart."

358

The other guys in Bob's foursome were getting a little annoyed.

"Come on, Bob," they complained. "It's getting late and we want to get home. Will you just concede the match, already?"

"I'll never concede the match, and besides," he said, leaning over his putt, "it's not all that late. Now will you all quit your complaining, and *please* hold that damn flashlight still."

359

A group of the boys were sitting in the locker room one afternoon.

"The toughest shot in golf," said the first guy, "is driving the last fairway, to win the U.S. Open."

"Nonsense," said the second guy. "The toughest shot in all of golf is a long-iron second shot, to win the British Open."

"That's ridiculous," said the third guy. "The toughest shot in all of golf is a pitch onto the eighteenth green at Augusta National, to win the Masters."

"You're all nuts!" said the fourth guy. "*The* toughest shot in all of golf is a three-foot putt, being watched by the guy sitting on the lawnmower, waiting to cut the green."

360

Golfer to buddy: "Did you know that those golf pros make more money than the President of the United States?"

Buddy to golfer: "That's only fair. They hit a lot fewer people when they play golf."

361

A senior partner from a New York law firm traveled to Japan to negotiate a municipal bond transaction. After a week of fifteen-hour working days, his Japanese host invited him to play a round of golf.

Not wishing to be an ungracious guest, he agreed to go along—but not without some trepidation, as he was a very serious man with precious little time for things such as golf.

Upon arrival at the course, he was introduced to a beautiful nineteen-year-old girl who would act as his guide for the day. As the round progressed, he found himself able to rise to the occasion. After each ball he hit, his guide let out a loud cry of "Assayo! Assayo!"

Thinking he was playing great golf, he continued to whack away, while she continued her cries of "Assayo! Assayo!"

Two weeks later, his Japanese counterpart flew to New York to close the bond deal. After a week of intense negotiations, the deal was finally closed. To return the hospitality he had enjoyed in Japan, he asked the Japanese lawyer what he would like to do the following day. The Japanese lawyer replied that he wanted to play a round of golf, since it was considered a luxury in his country.

The next morning, they got up early and headed out to the golf course. The Japanese lawyer was accorded the honors on the first tee, and proceeded to hit his drive three hundred fifteen yards down the center of the fairway, where it trickled onto the green of the par-four hole. Searching for a way to show how impressed he was with this shot, the American lawyer recalled the words expressed to him by his guide in Japan. He turned to the Japanese lawyer and blurted out "Assayo! Assayo!"

A dark and perplexed expression came across the face of the Japanese lawyer, who after looking once again down the fairway, turned to the American and said "What do you mean, *wrong hole?!*"

362

A woman out on the golf course hit her tee shot into the woods. She went in to retrieve it and stumbled across a magic lamp. She rubbed the magic lamp and a genie appeared.

"I'm going to grant you three wishes," said the genie. "But there's a catch."

"Isn't there always?" said the woman. "What is it?"

"Any of the wishes I grant you," said the genie, "I must also grant to your husband, ten times over."

"That miserable bum!" said the woman. "He doesn't deserve anything, but I guess I shouldn't cut off my nose to spite my face, so okay."

"What's your first wish?" asked the genie.

"I want a million dollars," said the lady.

"Okay," said the genie, "but remember, your husband will get ten times that amount."

"Who cares? For my second wish, I want to be the world's greatest female golfer," said the woman.

"No problem," said the genie, "but remember, your husband..."

"Fine!" she said. "And for my third wish..."

"Yes?" said the genie.

"For my third wish," she smiled, "give me an *itty-bitty* heart attack!"

A man receives a solicitation in the mail one day, inviting him to visit a golf resort where everything costs one dollar. The man jumps at the offer and heads off for a weekend of fun in the sun.

He arrives and plays a round of golf. It costs him a buck. When he goes for dinner that evening, it costs him another buck. He wakes the next morning in a room that also cost him one dollar. The day before he's to check out, he goes to play a last round of golf. Being almost out of balls, he stops in the pro shop and charges a sleeve of three balls to his room.

When he's checking out the next morning, he looks at his bill and sees "Golf: $1.00. Dinner: $1.00. Room: $1.00. Sleeve of golf balls: $3,000.00." He almost hits the ceiling!

Immediately calling over the manager, he asks, "What is this all about? Everything is supposed to cost one dollar, and you charge me three thousand for three crummy golf balls?"

"I'm sorry sir," said the manager, "but that's what our golf balls cost."

"Well, for goodness' sake," said the man. "If I wanted to spend that kind of money, I could've gone to the hotel across the street and paid them a thousand dollars a day for a room. At least then I would've known what I was paying for!"

"That's your prerogative, sir," said the manager. "Over there, they get you by the room. Here, we get you by the balls!"

364

First golfer: "I played with a guy the other day that was soooo short off the tee..."

Second golfer: "How short was he?"

First golfer: "He was so short, that when he asked me to check the yardage marker, all it said was 'Just Hit the Ball!'"

365

Pat came home from the golf course, fuming.

"I'll never play golf with that dog Ben again," he grumbled.

"What's the problem this time? asked his wife.

"I couldn't believe it," said Pat. "That bastard refused to concede a one-foot putt on the eighteenth hole."

"So what's the big deal?" she asked.

"What's the big deal?" snapped Pat, "It cost me *two strokes!*"

More Humor Books From Carol Publishing Group

Advanced Backstabbing and Mudslinging Techniques by George Hayduke, paperback $7.95 (#40560)

First, Kill All the Lawyers, compiled by Bill Adler, paper $8.95 (#51587)

Getting Even by George Hayduke, oversized paper $14.95 (#40314)

Getting Even 2 by George Hayduke, oversized paper $12.95 (#40337)

If New York City Was the World, by John Kerschbaum, paper $8.95 (#51573)

Make 'em Pay by George Hayduke, paper $8.95 (#40421)

Make My Day by George Hayduke, paper $8.95 (#40464)

Mayhem by George Hayduke, paper $7.95 (#40565)

Men Just Don't Understand: A Woman's Dating Dictionary by Nancy Linn-Desmond, paper $8.95 (#51666)

More of the World's Best Dirty Jokes by Mr. "J", paper $5.95 (#50710)

999 Lies For Every Occasion by Jo Donnelly, paper $8.95 (#51672)

"O'Brien and Fitzgerald Walk Into A Bar...": The World's Best Irish Jokes by Mr. "O's", paper $7.95 (#51663)

Revenge by George Hayduke, oversized paper $14.95 (#40353)

Revenge Tactics From the Master of Mayhem by George Hayduke, paper $8.95 (#40575)

Still More of the World's Best Dirty Jokes by Mr. "J", paper $3.95 (#50834)

365 Funniest Golf Jokes compiled by Fred Gefen, paper $9.95 (#51688)

"Three Rabbis In A Rowboat...": The World's Best Jewish Humor by A. Stanley Kramer, paper $9.95 (#51775)

201 Ways to Get Even With Your Boss by Linda Higgins, paper $8.95 (#51570)

Underground Office Humor by S.E. Mills, paper $9.95 (#51567)

The World's Dirtiest Dirty Jokes by Mr. "J", paper $7.95 (#51478)